FINDING #49

AND AMERICA'S FORGOTTEN MOTOCROSS TEAM

KEITH GEISNER

Archway Publishing books may be ordered through booksellers or by contacting:

Archway Publishing
1663 Liberty Drive
Bloomington, IN 47403
www.archwaypublishing.com
1 (888) 242-5904

Because of the dynamic nature of the internet, any web addresses or links contained in this book may have changed since publication and may no longer be valid. The views expressed in this work are solely those of the author and do not necessarily reflect the views of the publisher, and the publisher hereby disclaims any responsibility for them.

Photography by Cycle News, Jim Gianatsis/FastDates.com, Mark Wick, Debbie Morgan, Lyndon Fox, John Brier, Mark Kiel, Harley-Davidson Archives, Joseph Savant, Phil Davy, Steve Gustafson, James LaPaz, Craig Mueller, Jay Clark, AMA Pro, Terry Nichols, Tracy Nichols, Barcroft Media Limited, Doug Hill, Jeff Holzhausen, Tommy Montgomery and Keith Geisner.

ISBN: 978-1-4808-8252-2 (sc)
ISBN: 978-1-4808-8254-6 (hc)
ISBN: 978-1-4808-8253-9 (e)

Library of Congress Control Number: 2019915272

Print information available on the last page.

Archway Publishing rev. date: 11/14/2019

ACKNOWLEDGEMENTS

I would like to thank the Harley-Davidson motocross team members, photographers, and everyone else whose names appear throughout the pages of the book for helping me tell this story. I would also like to say a special thanks to my wife, Sara, for supporting me during this journey.

CONTENTS

PREFACE

How often does one win the lottery? I'm not talking about Powerball or Mega Millions. How many times has something you are deeply passionate about entered your life unexpectedly? That is the true lottery.

I know—I experienced it.

I was the guy in the transportation section of Barnes & Noble devouring every book on motorcycles I could find; the guy watching every episode of *American Pickers* just waiting to see which rare motorcycle Mike and Frank would come across next—all while dreaming of the day when I would find a special motorcycle in a barn.

That is exactly what happened one sunny September afternoon in 2016. Only I didn't just find a special motorcycle in a barn—as my friend Ray Mungenast would later say, a special motorcycle in a barn found me. It came in the form of a dirt bike, and not just any dirt bike. It was a rare piece of Harley-Davidson motocross history.

Between 1975 and 1978 something unheard-of happened in the sport of lightweight motocross racing: Harley-Davidson, America's number one manufacturer of heavyweight, air-cooled motorcycles, entered the competition....

INTRODUCTION

I've been into motorcycles for as long as I can remember. One of my earliest memories was of my uncle racing hare scrambles in southeastern Missouri. I would be at my grandparents' house when he would return home from a race and would drool over his Honda XR500. Sitting on the bike, my short legs dangling, only fueled my passion.

Later, when I was ten, my fourteen-year-old twin brothers Jeff and John and I all received new dirt bikes. My brothers' bikes were 1986 Suzuki DR125s, and mine was an '86 DR100. By then we had been riding the rolling farmland on Yamaha GT80s and go-carts.

From the beginning, I was intrigued by things with motors and how they worked. Since my father was a car guy, my older brothers and I learned all about small gas engines. We learned how to do maintenance on our motorcycles, from tightening the chains or cleaning the air filters to changing the tires. In high school I learned to rebuild suspensions and motors with the help of an uncle and another friend of the family. I had plenty of mentors.

Around this same time, I caught the bug for making money from fixing up dirt bikes and reselling them. I always kept an eye on the classified ads and often picked up bikes to flip. This experience exposed me to many different types of bikes. I had to research the bikes I fixed up in order to know how to price and market them. In the meantime, I also became pretty good at shopping for parts. I'd make a list of motorcycle parts suppliers listed in the back of *Dirt Bike* magazine and then call each one to compare prices and negotiate the best deals. Even though I didn't own a bike shop, I'd act like I was a shop owner and use fake customer scenarios to leverage prices and faster shipping. In time I became well-versed in the various makes and models of motorcycles.

My parents also owned an automotive collision repair business, so I had every color of paint at my disposal. It was easy for me to touch up a bike and make it look brand new.

Before I graduated from high school, I told my parents I wanted to attend the Motorcycle Mechanic Institute, but they told me I needed to go to college and get a four-year degree. I took their advice and attended Southeast Missouri State University. While in college, I collected over a hundred Honda Z50s and CT70s. I stored them all at my parents' place, but when I moved to St. Louis after college, it was time for them to go. I ended up selling the whole lot to a collector in Minnesota. That trailer-load of Honda minis leaving my parents' house was quite a sight!

Around 1997 I started using the internet to buy, sell, and research motorcycles; my knowledge of motorcycles and motorcycle sales grew exponentially. Up until that time, I'd been limited to buying from magazines and newspapers. The internet raised the bar considerably. Not only did I visit and join online motorcycle swap meets, but I also helped my dad sell a surplus of cars and parts he had collected over the years. He got a kick out of me learning the ins and outs of online motorcycle sales. He also marveled at the weekly flow of money orders and cashier's checks in the mail.

In 1999, eBay changed my entire business strategy. I now had an easier way to sell parts. I invested in a new computer and purchased my first digital camera. This really expanded my ability to make money and support my hobby.

After I graduated college in 1999, I became an engineer in the automotive and aviation industries. I also got into racing hare scrambles and vintage motocross and riding a Harley-Davidson Dyna Wide Glide. The latter ended with a bad accident in 2010, but I still enjoy off-road racing and continue to buy, sell, collect, and restore motorcycles. The joy I get out of bringing a vintage bike back to life is something few would understand. I always keep my eyes peeled for a rarity or a good deal.

I am now in my forties and my passion for "everything motorcycle" has yet to subside. That same passion also compelled me to share this story....

CHAPTER 1

I first came across the Harley-Davidson motocross bike on a Friday evening in September 2016. It was getting late, and before I went to bed, I pulled up Craigslist on my iPhone to see what deals were out there.

When I first saw the Harley-Davidson MX250 ad, I thought to myself, *There's a rare bike you don't see every day.* At that point I knew very little about the 1978 Harley-Davidson MX250. What I did know was that around 1,000 were sold to the public and that restored ones were going anywhere from $6,000 to $10,000. I emailed the seller a reasonable offer before I texted my buddy Jeff Allison, a fellow vintage bike enthusiast, and asked if he had seen the same ad.

Jeff and I loved to hunt for deals on cool, collectible stuff. To be more specific, we focused mostly on anything related to motorcycles. That's how Jeff and I first met. Even though we lived five minutes apart and had mutual friends, we were first introduced over a motorcycle deal. I had a BSA chopper project that Jeff wanted, and he offered me a pretty good trade to get the deal made. The rest is history.

Needless to say, when I spied the Harley-Davidson MX250 on Craigslist, I had to share the discovery with Jeff. After texting him, I did something that I rarely did: I double-checked the email I had sent to the seller. I discovered that I had messed up my cell number, so I sent a second email. (I often think of what might have happened, or not have happened, if I had not double-checked my email that night.)

The next morning, I got a phone call from the seller accepting my offer. He had done his research and knew what the bike was worth restored and was tired of all the low-ball offers he'd been getting. I told him to remove the bike from Craigslist so people would stop contacting him and made plans to meet him the next afternoon. The bike was at his father's farm in Shelbina, Missouri, and he had to go and get it. This worked out well for me because I had planned on racing the Kenda AMA National Enduro the next morning at St. Joe State Park in Park Hills, Missouri, and by the time it was over the seller would be ready for me. Meanwhile, I was excited. I had never owned a Harley-Davidson MX250 and I was looking forward to the restoration.

Meanwhile, Jeff called and said that someone had posted a picture of the Craigslist ad on a well-known Facebook page that identified and appraised motocross dirt bikes. The bike I was buying might be a factory team bike, he said. I was totally floored as I searched out the Facebook page in question. The post was blowing up with a long thread of comments. Various people were weighing in on the bike having parts or traits that weren't "production." The bike's features were those of a factory team bike. The most intriguing part of the bike was its number plate: 49. I discovered that #49 belonged to Don "Killer" Kudalski, the last rider to race for the Harley-Davidson MX team, who had also graced the cover of *Cycle News* for being the only rider to win a major AMA race for the team.

CYCLE NEWS

EAST

Volume XII : Number 7 : March 1, 1978 75¢

Kudalski doubles-up in Florida Winter-AMA Series; scores first major MX win for H-D

***

Ellis is king of Seattle Kingdome Supercross

***

Vesterinen wins World Championship Trials opener

***

Hurricane Hannah tells you how to do it

***

A short burst on Kawasaki's 250 works replica

***

Ice racing, words from Roger D, New Products, Daytona contest, Motocross Cat, Goin' For It, and much more!

NEWSPAPER

Don "Killer" Kudalski #49 making Harley-Davidson history. Photo provided by *Cycle News*.

My heart was jumping out of my chest. To think that I could possibly be the owner of a factory team bike was unimaginable. I couldn't wait to see the bike live and up close. Jeff was as excited as I was. He insisted that I go and get the bike immediately, but I couldn't since the seller didn't have it in his possession yet. To help me sleep that night, I emailed the seller and told him that I was still game and looking forward to meeting him the next day. Thankfully, he confirmed with an email saying the same. I banked on his honesty and slept well that night.

When I told my wife, Sara, about the bike, she was happy for me, knowing my love of vintage motorcycles. I kept her up to date on what I was learning about the bike's possible history. I informed her that the Harley-Davidson MX team also had a rider by the name of Rex Staten. Our son's name is Rex—anything to help me pull another bike into the garage.

Rex Staten #31, 1977 Daytona Supercross. Photo by Jim Gianatsis/FastDates.com.

Sunday morning came and I loaded up to race the Kenda AMA National Enduro at St. Joe State Park. I was meeting some friends from work and we had a bet going that the slowest time had to pay for lunch on Monday. I told them about the Harley-Davidson MX250 and my plans for picking it up after the race. It was my excuse for going slower that day so as not to have a wreck and miss out on purchasing a possible piece of motorcycle history. I was sure the bike would be worth the price of lunch for my friends.

The race was fun, but I was anxious to head home and then hit the road. I gave Jeff a call and asked if he wanted to ride along with me to pick up the MX bike. He eagerly agreed, and soon we were headed to central Missouri. On the way, we thought of a list of questions we wanted to ask the seller.

We finally made it to the destination, which was a commuter parking lot off the interstate. As I approached the seller's truck, he jumped out and introduced himself. I noticed right away he was carrying a pistol. He made it known that he always took precautions when dealing with strangers on Craigslist. I told him I didn't blame him and that we didn't want any trouble. The first question I asked him was why he was selling the bike. He told me he didn't ride motorcycles and the bike had been sitting in his father's barn since the mid-1980s. The bike was given to him by his father. He and his dad had tried to get it running at one time, but the parts were hard to find. He specifically mentioned the rear sprocket, which was off the bike and in a box of parts.

When Jeff and I inquired about the number 49 on the bike, he said he wasn't sure and had always assumed his dad had put them on. When I mentioned that the bike appeared to have parts from the Harley-Davidson MX factory race team, he didn't seem interested in the least. He didn't ride, and he was married with young children.

All the way home, Jeff and I discussed the bike's possible history. I looked into a website called msolisvintagemotorcycles.com that contained a lot of information about the Harley-Davidson MX race team, including detailed photos of bikes and their riders. When I got the bike home, I put the number plates on correctly and took several pictures, preparing for my research.

That evening, I visited the Vintage Motocross Buyers & Sellers Price Guide Facebook page and let everyone know I ended up with the bike and that my goal was to research its origin and decide its fate.

#49 just arrived at its new home. Photo by Keith Geisner.

CHAPTER 2

THE RESEARCH BEGINS

To begin my research, I used three valuable internet sites that helped me find 90 percent of my information: Google, Facebook, and Anywho.com. Most people are familiar with Google and Facebook, but Anywho.com might not be a readily recognizable site to some readers.

Anywho.com allows you to search by name, city, and state for anyone who has or had a landline (home phone). It will give you their phone numbers and addresses. My research started with the seller. If my bike was a factory Harley-Davidson team bike, how did it make it to Missouri? I started googling the owner's name and found that he had three brothers. What I found interesting was that his brothers had a different last name. I then searched the seller's Facebook profile and confirmed these individuals were his brothers. I didn't want to bug the seller yet, so I reached out to his brothers through Facebook to see what they knew of the dirt bike.

While I waited for their replies, I wanted to know more about the barn in Shelbina where the bike had been stored. I found the father's name via Facebook and was able to get his home phone number and address from Anywho.com. The phone number was no longer in service, so I contacted a neighbor, also through Anywho.com, and left a message for them to pass on to the father. Within an hour, I got responses from the brothers and the father. One of the brothers informed me that the seller was actually a stepbrother and that the dirt bike had belonged to his biological father. The stepfather confirmed the story and said that the bike had been stored in his barn in Shelbina since the mid-'80s.

It turned out that all my investigating was making the family a little nervous, which in hindsight, I can understand. A couple of the brothers were pissed off that I was contacting various family members. I explained that I meant no harm and was only trying to research the bike's history. Finally, the previous owner contacted me and, after telling me to tone it down a little, told me he would reach out to his father for more information about the bike. I was fine with that, as his biological father was the man I wanted to speak to anyway. The seller also sent me a photo of him and his dad on the bike. He told me that when his parents divorced, his dad had given him the bike to keep, and that's how it ended up in the stepfather's barn in Shelbina.

I was impatient and instead of waiting to hear from the seller's father, I hit the internet again after finding out the man's name. Through searching my usual sites I finally contacted the stepmother. This time, I was careful in how I began my conversation, making it clear that I had purchased the bike from her husband's son and that I was only researching the history of a motorcycle. She told me to call back later when he would be home. When I called him that evening, he said that he never raced the bike but had used it as a farm bike. He said that he had bought it in its current condition from a motorcycle shop in Shelbina, Missouri, after tagging along with a buddy who was shopping for a three-wheeler. The Harley-Davidson caught his eye and the owner let him take it home for some test-riding. He was so impressed with the bike's power that he bought it and kept it until he eventually gave it to his son.

After hearing his story, my next mission was to find out about the bike shop in Shelbina….

I started my next search on Google Maps and began searching the Shelbina area for any motorcycle shops—there were none. I began to consider what businesses would still be around that had probably existed in the early 80s. I thought of my hometown and the local Missouri Farmers Association. I looked up the number for Shelbina's local agricultural store and sure enough, there was an old guy who worked there who remembered the bike shop. The name of the shop was Tricky Dick's and the owner was a man by the name of Jerry Lillard. To my amazement, Jerry was still working out of the same building, but he was now an insurance agent. I googled "Tricky Dick's", hoping to get all my questions answered.

As a result of my search I learned that Tricky Dick's specialized in converting a version of the Cagiva brand dirt bike into a custom race three-wheeler. What was significant about Cagiva? Cagiva was created after Harley-Davidson sold off its Italian motorcycle division, Aermacchi, in 1978. Cagiva took the 1978 Harley-Davidson MX250, made a few design changes, and began selling it as the 1979 Cagiva MXR and RX. It now made sense to me why the owner had this bike in his shop at the time.

I phoned Jerry Lillard's office and spoke with his receptionist, who informed me that Jerry was out for a few days. She did give me his cell phone number, however, and in my anxiety to learn about the bike, I ended up calling him. Jerry was kind enough to talk to me briefly, informing me that he did recall having a couple of such bikes in his shop, but that he had no memory of one with #49 on it. He also confirmed that he knew the previous owner of the MX250 in my possession, but insisted that the guy did not purchase that bike from him. To say the least, I was disappointed.

I phoned the former owner again and told him what Jerry had told me. He swore up and down that the bike had been purchased at Tricky Dick's. I thanked him for his time and told him I'd send him some photos when the restoration was complete. In the meantime, my mind was working overtime: I had two conflicting stories and my trail had gone cold. Was one of them mistaken? Had the bike been stolen? I checked with my Missouri Vintage MX contacts in Moberly and Kansas City and the bike didn't ring a bell. I then decided to change direction and focus my research on what was known about #49 and who might still be around from the time the bike was being raced.

CHAPTER 3

SEARCHING FOR CLUES

There were many similarities between my bike and the team bikes I reviewed on the internet. I learned that in 1977 the team had used frames built by Jeff Cole from C&J, and all the plastic was made by Hoss Industries. Everything checked out with my bike. The seat was very similar to the ones I viewed and even the front number plate on my bike had the same plastic mounting bracket that wrapped around the fork tubes. I noticed some had black handlebars and some had chrome. They all used Magura levers and a special tank strap—mine had a stock production tank strap. The MX250s all had left-hand-exiting exhausts and the tank petcocks were relocated to the right-hand side. The fork reliefs were either beat in with a hammer or cut out, flipped and re-welded to create a relief in the tank. Along with the production tank strap, I discovered from the VIN number on the motor that my bike also had a production motor. The rear shocks were production Harley-Davidson MX as well, so something fishy was going on. Why was there a mixture of production and team parts on this bike?

Besides the VIN on the motor, the only other number was a six-digit serial number stamped on the steering neck, D87840. This mystery frame number took some time to figure out—more on that later. The one major difference I noticed between my bike and the bikes ridden by the Harley-Davidson MX team was the shape of my side number plates. The side number plates on my bike were squared off on the lower rear corners, versus the other team bikes whose plates had rounded corners. The only other team bike that had number plates similar to mine was the water-cooled MX bike on display at the Harley-Davidson Museum in Milwaukee, Wisconsin. I found several photos of this bike online and, aside from the water-cooled motor and radiator, the two bikes were similar. What really got my attention, though, was the six-digit serial number on the frame of the museum bike.

The water-cooled team bike located at the Harley-Davidson museum had the same shaped side number plates as #49. Photo by Mark Wick.

Notice the serial number on the down tube of the frame, below the steering stop. Photo by Mark Wick.

Serial number found on the frame: D87840. Photo by Keith Geisner.

I located the Harley-Davidson Museum Facebook page and sent them an instant message about the bike I had found. I did get a response, but instead of background information on #49, I received advice and recommendations on restoration services. I decided to phone the museum to see if I could get someone to answer my questions live. I ended up connecting with the lead tour guide director—more on that later.

The night I brought the bike home, I joined Tom Fox's Harley-Davidson MX Owners Facebook Group. Tom Fox was a local guy I knew from the vintage MX scene in Missouri. He had previously owned a production Harley-Davidson MX250 and had put together the online group as a source of information and parts. I hoped that by posting pics of #49 and telling my story I might get some leads in researching the bike's history.

Some members knew what parts made up the Harley-Davidson MX team bikes and that my bike had a lot of these parts, but no one knew anything about the frame serial number or how the bike made its way to Missouri. I continued to use the group as my home base for updates on the bike's progress and information I had gleaned. Each time I posted something, I hoped that the latest update might jog someone's memory on team bikes.

It was on this Facebook page that I first got introduced to Mason Boyd. Mason lived in Florida and had been in touch with #49's rider, Don "Killer" Kudalski. Mason's comment, "Let me ask Killer about your bike," really caught my attention.

Mason had raced a hybrid version of the production Harley-Davidson MX250 in the Florida Vintage MX series. He shared pictures of my bike with Don right away. He also shared a photo of Don that he believed his father had taken. It was good to know I now had a connection to an original Harley-Davidson MX team rider. I would end up talking with Mason many times in the coming months.

The photo of Don Kudalski that Mason shared with me. 1978 Winter-AMA. Photo by Debbie Morgan.

There was another Facebook page that became a useful tool in my search. On the day I struck the deal on #49, as I mentioned earlier, my good friend Jeff had seen someone posting the bike on a well-known vintage bike page called Vintage Motocross Buyers & Sellers Price Guide. The page owner was a guy named Joe Abbate.

Joe owned a motorcycle restoration business called Cycle Therapy and was heavily involved in the vintage MX scene. When I brought the bike home, I visited Joe's page and read the comment thread on the bike. This information proved useful to me and I ended up posting that I had purchased the bike. I received a nice reply from Joe, and I followed up by commenting on how much I had paid for the MX—after all, the page was for determining the value of such motorcycles. I received several positive comments on my purchase.

In the next two to three weeks, I would reach out to Joe for his input on what direction I should go with the bike. Should I do a full-up restoration, or should I preserve as much as I could? With Joe's feedback, I took the preservation route. He told me to "rub on that bike until your fingers bleed" and to get all the documentation I could along the way. He also told me to take care in preserving the paint. I owe Joe a great debt of gratitude for his direction and assistance.

I discovered only one website that featured bikes, parts, and previous team members. The site's owner was Menalco Solis III. I reached out to him during the first week of my search and he helped me to identify the production motor in #49. He had posted a story on his website about the Harley-Davidson MX team bike that he owned and where it had come from. He did a great job capturing the history of the MX team.

Menalco and I hit it off right away and in the next year would assist one another in our restorations. We would also solve a few mysteries surrounding the Harley-Davidson MX team and bring to light a wealth of information that needed to be recorded and preserved.

My new *American Motorcyclist* magazine arrived in November and it listed the 2016 inductees into the AMA Hall of Fame. To my surprise, Jeff Cole of C&J was on the list. I had had no idea he was still around, but this news gave me hope that I might find some answers about my bike's frame.

I searched Facebook and found a group for C&J-framed motorcycles. I quickly joined the page and posted a photo of #49, asking for any answers as to the mystery serial number on the steering neck. I got a surprising response: Jeff Cole's phone number.

When I called the number, Jeff himself answered, and I was immediately unnerved to be speaking with an icon in the motorcycle industry. I told him about my bike and asked if he recalled how many frames he had built for the Harley-Davidson MX team. He replied that he thought he had built between six and ten frames, but no more than that. When I mentioned the serial number on my frame, he had no recollection of stamping any serial numbers on team frames. I thanked him for his time, happy to at least know how many frames he had built for the MX team.

At this early stage of finding the #49 bike, I had a small list of parts the bike needed in order to be complete. I wasn't totally sure of what I needed, or what direction I needed to go, so I just started looking for anything related to the Harley-Davidson MX250.

Dave Griffin was a co-worker who shared my enthusiasm for motorcycles. He rode his BMW GS1200 to work daily and we engaged in bike talk every chance we got. After hearing about my find, he began keeping an eye out for parts. He told me of a place near Eureka Springs, Arkansas, that stocked a lot of Aermacchi parts. I did a Google search and found the small bike shop, which was known as 39 Cycles. I phoned the shop mid-week and left a message, and that following weekend I got a return call from Rich, the owner.

I told Rich I was looking for anything related to the MX250 and he said he would check and get back to me. A week later I got a call from Rich and his wife, Sue. They informed me that they had a few new old stock (NOS) cylinders and a couple of heads. Sue would send me photos and we would go from there. When the photos arrived, I was in shock. They had four 1975 MX250 cylinders with one perfect 1975 MX250 head and a damaged 1978 MX250 head with cylinder. As the story goes, only 100 1975 H-D MX250s were ever produced. They were the bikes with forks used for the rear shocks. I knew these parts were rare, and even though they didn't go on my bike, I had to get them.

We agreed on a price and Sue sent the parts to me by FedEx. I was officially in the parts business, but there was more to these MX cylinders than I imagined, and the parts played an important role in the research and completion of #49.

Another MX parts purchase I made came from Facebook. I joined a couple of groups that focused on Harley-Davidson and Aermacchi motorcycles. A gentleman in Italy was selling a bunch of NOS production parts to a 1978 MX. Most of the parts were only for a production bike, but some of the engine parts I could use on mine. I reached out to the man and purchased an NOS production seat, NOS production rear sprocket, and several other items that would come in handy if I needed to barter. Aermacchi bikes were manufactured in Italy, so these parts had likely never left the country. It was my first of several overseas parts purchases.

CHAPTER 4

FINDING THE TEAM

I began to wonder just how many team members were still living and how many I might be able to locate. My first successful contact was with team member Don Habermehl. I got Don's name from Menalco's website. He had been the lead mechanic for the MX team from 1975 through 1977. Initially, I sent him a friend request through Facebook, but I ended up connecting with his son, John. I had messaged John as well, explaining who I was and that I had recently bought an MX team bike. I also included some photos of the bike. I got a response in no time, and John told me that the bike looked familiar. He reflected on the days when he was young and his father had been the team mechanic and told me that he would pass on my information to his dad.

A few days later, I got a phone call from Don. I was both nervous and excited to be speaking with an original team mechanic. I struggled to keep my cool so that I could sound professional and informed about what I had discovered about #49 thus far.

I asked Don about the serial number, but he didn't recall any. I then inquired if the production motor could have made its way through the race department and onto a team bike, to which he replied that he was doubtful that could have happened. When I asked if he had any photos from his racing days, he told me that they had been too busy to take pictures. I could tell I was challenging Don's memory—after all, it had been forty years. He was gracious enough to give me his email address so that I could send him some pictures of the bike. He also gave me the contact information for the team's former lead project engineer, John Ingham. It was John who gave Don his start with the Harley-Davidson MX team.

John was the lead project engineer for the MX team from 1975 to 1978 and the lead designer of the Aermacchi SX Enduro models going back to 1972. It was in 1972 that he and others first saw Don Habermehl racing a Honda S90 at a local MX track and at local endurance races. Harley-Davidson had its West Coast division develop a 100cc bike for the Baja, and John, through some communication with a gentleman named Dick O'Brien, persuaded Don to ride the bike. Don rode the Baja in MX races at local tracks until he had an accident that knocked him unconscious. After that, he thought he might be better off sticking with endurance racing. At some point, Don was between jobs and John was looking for someone to test-ride the SX175, a project that he was developing. John managed to get a bike and he and Don did some racing together.

John Ingham spoke with the people at Harley-Davidson, trying to get them to hire Don as a test rider. It was supposedly a go until the union test riders protested. The R&D shop supervisor then said he would hire Don as a mechanic to work on the prototype for the MX. That was when Don officially began his work with Harley-Davidson.

Don with Marty Tripes at the 1977 Winter-AMA. Photo by Jim Gianatsis/FastDates.com.

They cleaned out a work area in the R&D department and moved the frame—and Don—in. The operation was there for many months before there was talk of moving the operation to the racing department. Don asked if he could move with it, and in 1973-74 his wish was granted: John would get the frames and parts shipped in and Don would assemble them into prototypes. John would also contact local riders and they would test the prototypes. This went on until 1978, when Harley-Davidson decided to pull the plug on MX racing. After the '77 season, Don began work on the XR750 in the racing department. He worked on everything from engine builds to tire changes, but ignitions were his specialty. One of his biggest projects was the XR1000 Lucifer's Hammer. Don came up with the idea of mounting the oil tank under the frame. He was with Harley-Davidson until 1985 when, along with most of the team, he was laid off.

When I initially contacted John Ingham with all my questions, his reaction was somewhat the same as Don's: "It was forty years ago...hard to remember...." John gave me his email and I sent him some photos of the bike. He readily responded and said that it was definitely a team bike, but that he couldn't place it. He told me the bike was a model from the later years of the team's heyday, and that the exhaust was also from that era. The clutch basket with the safety-wired snap ring was not familiar, but then again, he said, "Marty Tripes was pretty hard on clutches." John also told me they had made a few different sets of triple clamps and that Don "Killer" Kudalski had crashed in Florida due to a broken triple clamp. All of this information gave me great hope that I could find out more about #49 and its history—and, thanks to John, I found another bread crumb on the trail in the form of former team manager Clyde Denzer.

Clyde couldn't offer me much information, but he always encouraged me and passed along my queries to anyone involved with the MX team or its history. He always responded to my emails and was courteous and supportive. I was grateful. Although I thought I had hit a bit of a dead end I was about to get an assist from another source.

In my conversations with Don Habermehl, he had also mentioned a former team engineer named Rex Marsee. I searched Facebook and finally got in contact with a nephew, who gave me Rex's phone number. Rex was delighted to talk with me about my recent acquisition.

Rex's work with the Harley-Davidson MX team was early in the development of the 1975 MX250. He also helped design the production MX bikes that H-D sold in 1975. When I asked Rex about the serial number on my frame, he came back with the first real answer that made sense: it was a date and sequence number, "D878" meaning "Date August 1978" and "40" being the sequence of the frame. Rex added that this was only a guess of course, and that by the time Kudalski was racing, Rex would have no longer been with the company. Still, I knew roughly how many frames Jeff Cole had designed, and I was getting closer and closer to an answer.

Rex was first discovered by Harley-Davidson after he designed and built his own motorcycle that was featured in a September 1974 edition of *Cycle News*. The bike was built ahead of its time, so much so that over a decade later both Buell and Victory would have a similar design. The bike was called the Marsee Magnum, and Rex said that article had kicked off his motorcycle career. After leaving Harley-Davidson, Rex went on to start his own line of motorcycle riding gear and luggage. Rex's roots run deep in the industry, and I was excited to make his acquaintance. At the time I met him, he was in the process of writing his autobiography.

The sand-cast magnesium frame eliminates many of the bolt on components found on a conventional machine: gas tank, rear fender brackets, etc.

Rex Marsee's *Cycle News* article. Photo provided by *Cycle News*.

It was mid-December 2016 and I bugged Don Habermehl enough to allow me to send him a picture to autograph. This was part of the documentation of my research. I also reached out to John Ingham and they both agreed to sign photos.

The photo I sent to Don to sign was a picture of him with John along with Al Unser inside the H-D race department, looking at MX250 cylinders. The picture I sent to John was a photo of him and Rex Staten standing next to Rex's 1977 #31 team bike. About a week after I mailed Don's photo, I was at my brother's house for a Christmas party. My cell rang and I saw it was a Milwaukee number: it was Don Habermehl, calling to ask where on the photo I would like him to sign. He had already signed the border, but he wanted to be sure. I told him that having his signature anywhere on the photograph was fine with me, and he signed it once more, next to his picture. Before we ended the call, he told me of another mechanic who had traveled with Kudalski during the 1978 season, after Habermehl was pulled off the MX team and assigned to another part of the racing department. The mechanic's name was Tom Volin.

The next day, I contacted John Ingham to confirm Don's story. John remembered where Tom was from and I did my usual search on Anywho.com. I located Tom's phone number and left a message. A few days later, I got a call.

Tom Volin with #31 Rex Staten. Photo by Lyndon Fox.

After I relayed my story and my affiliation with Habermehl and Ingham, Tom confirmed that he had been with the H-D MX team during the 1977-78 season and had also been with Kudalski in the final '78 run. At first, Tom seemed certain that I had a production bike, because he had been instructed to destroy some bikes at the end of the season. He had actually taken a hacksaw to some frames. He said that he had urged Harley-Davidson to put the bikes in the museum, but his pleas had fallen on deaf ears. When I started naming off a few of #49's features, his tune changed. He said it sounded like I had a factory works bike. I asked if he had any photos, and he had his wife, Kathy, send them on her iPhone. These were the clearest pictures of Don "Killer" Kudalski on his bike I had ever seen. They were black and white and in sharp detail. There was also a photograph of the team's RV, which had "Kudalski and 'Volinski'" painted on the side. Tom said that they had altered his name and referred to them as the "Polish race team."

#49 Don "Killer" Kudalski Winter-AMA at St. Petersburg, FL. Photo by Jim Gianatsis/FastDates.com.

This was the first knowledge I had of the motorhome. John Ingham gave me some information about the last motorhome used by the team: "That was right after I bought the Kings Highway motorhome. It was a nice unit, with the workshop in the back and lounge up front. Carried lots of spares housed in cabinets and tie-downs for the bikes. Kings Highway guys were late in finishing the unit, so we missed Hangtown to show the unit off. Everybody else was still using box vans to support the teams. We were initially known as the Hertz racing team, as that was what Don got to drive around to all the race venues the first year. He was much relieved to get the motorhome. The only failure on the unit was you had to rework the engine oil pump after each oil change, but Don got real good at that chore!"

Tom Volin also noted that he had raced before becoming a mechanic. I found proof of this when I located his name in *Cycle News* when he was racing for Husqvarna. Tom's Husqvarna experience would carry over to the H-D MX team.

1971 Delta Race, #47 Tom Volin lining up to race his Husqvarna. Photo by John Brier.

I was thrilled to have contacted a total of five team members and to have some awesome photos to study. My search for #49's origins was moving along at a steady pace, and I couldn't have been more pleased. When the signed photos from Don and John arrived, I was like a kid at Christmas. I got an even bigger surprise from John Ingham; along with his autographed photo was a Harley-Davidson MX team shirt. My wife recalled that she had never seen me smile like I did when I unfolded the shirt. The year 2017 was off to an incredible start—and I knew exactly whom I was going to contact next....

John Ingham surprised me with a team T-shirt. Photo by Keith Geisner.

As I wrote earlier, Mason Boyd owned a production model 1978 Harley-Davidson and lived and raced in Florida. He was my first connection to team rider Don "Killer" Kudalski. Don had supplied Mason with some photos of the bike he raced. Later, I sent Mason a photo for Don to sign, but I had to wait until Mason's schedule opened up and he could pay the former MX rider a visit.

Of course, my impatient side prevailed and I tried to contact Kudalski on my own. I found him through Facebook and contacted his wife, dropping Mason Boyd's name as a reference, as I noticed that he was a Facebook friend of hers. My message went like this: "My name is Keith Geisner and I've been speaking with Mason Boyd about a Harley-Davidson MX motorcycle that Don may have encountered in his racing days. I've been researching the bike and the Harley-Davidson team engineers and mechanics. I've been sharing my findings with Mason. I hope you don't mind me contacting you directly. I have some photos of Don that he may have never seen that I received from his last mechanic, Tom Volin. Without bugging you too much, do you mind if I keep you informed of my research? I was the guy who found that video of Don racing from the Harley-Davidson Museum. Take care, Keith."

To my excitement, Don himself responded: "Hello Keith; It's Don Kudalski, thanks for the shout out! I wish I could help with your research, but I would have no idea what exact bike I rode back then, but Tom Volin would know. Contact me anytime on my wife's page. Thanks for the research, I love it. Keep up the good work. Your friend, Don "Killer" Kudalski."

Don and I exchanged a few messages but his memories of his days with the MX team were foggy. He did remember a little, though. I shared the recent photos from Tom Volin and they jarred his memory. Don agreed to sign my photographs and he eventually requested copies for his wife and grandkids. I sent Don seven posters of the picture I had received from Tom. He commented that now his grandkids would know what he looked like when he had hair!

Not only did Don sign my photos, but he also sent me a nice letter: "Keith - Thanks for the pictures! Brings back a lot of memories! My family will enjoy them; keep up the good work on our bike! Please send pictures when it is done. God Bless, Don "Killer" Kudalski, #49."

Later on, I would ask Don how he got the name Killer, and this is what he said: "I started riding a Rokon in the 1974 Winter-AMA series in Florida. I kicked butt, so they hired me full time. I almost beat Tony DiStefano in the open class for the overall that winter. I then rode the Astrodome Supercross that same year in the open class. In the first moto I was running in the top three. Jimmy Wienert, the #1 plate, tried to pass me in a corner by stuffing me, but the Rokon was heavy and I held my ground. Jimmy went down, got up and finally passed me. After the moto in the pits Jimmy came over and said 'Hey, you see that #1 plate on my bike? Let me by!' And I said 'That's from last year—you have to earn that this year!' He shook his head and jokingly said 'You're a Killer!' That's how I got that nickname, Don "Killer" Kudalski."

Rex Staten was the Harley-Davidson MX team rider with the most hours on a team bike. He raced during the 1976 and 1977 seasons for Harley-Davidson. I was able to reach out to Rex through Facebook messaging. Rex, like the rest of the team, had a hard time remembering anything about my bike. Throughout the preservation I would share pictures with Rex, hoping it would jog his memory or get a discussion going.

One day, after picking my kids up from day care, I was looking through their arts and crafts for the day. My son Rex had created a picture of a rocket ship with his name on it. I shared a picture of it with Rex Staten and he got a kick out of it, since one of his nicknames was "Rocket Rex." Later on that week, Rex called me out of the blue and spoke about his days on the team. It was so cool of Rex to reach out to me and I'll never forget it.

Scott Wallenberg was a test rider and a member of the team for a short while. I found his name through my research on the MX team on Facebook. When I sent him an instant message, he responded quickly.

It was Rex Marsee who had reached out to Scott all those years ago, asking if he wanted to be a test rider for the production MX250 "non-race" team. Scott spent a lot of time test-riding the 1975 version of the MX bike, along with Pat Keller, who worked in the production department.

Scott provided several awesome photos of the team in the early days, taken by his father, Wally Wallenberg. Scott was a valuable source whenever I had questions during the restoration of #49.

Rex Staten #46 at the 1976 Saddleback Trans-AMA. Photo by Mark Kiel.

Rex #31 and Tom, 1977 Winter-AMA series. Photo by Jim Gianatsis/FastDates.com.

Rex #31 1977 Team Photo. Used with permission of the Harley-Davidson Archives.

1977 Winter-AMA, Tom and Rex. Photo by Lyndon Fox.

Ricky O'Brien got hooked up with the Harley-Davidson MX team after Eric Skrudland left in the early rounds of the 1976 Winter AMA series. (More on Eric Skrudland later.) According to Ricky, there was still a lot of trial and error going on with the bikes. He was a big Honda fan, so anything CR that he could make work on the team bike, he would. Tim Dixon was his mechanic. He and Tim were always trying different parts from other bikes to improve handling and performance, from pipes to suspension. Ricky said that one time they made so many changes on a bike that the team almost didn't let him ride it at the St. Peters, Missouri, race. At the end of the race, Dick O'Brien (no relation) asked that Ricky and his dad, Jay O'Brien, bring the bike up to the race department for review on the following Monday—that was the last they saw of the bike. Jay told me that upon comparing lap times on Ricky at a local track, they found that the Harley MX250 they modified was faster than Ricky's time on his Honda CR.

I had managed to track down Ricky through his sister, Terri. I also got to speak with Jay, his father. Jay was always Ricky's mechanic no matter what team he raced for. He told me that Tim Dixon and Rex Staten were frequent houseguests when Ricky was on the team. After Ricky's MX racing career ended, he got into professional stock car racing.

Ricky O'Brien was #76 when racing for the Harley-Davidson MX team in 1976. Photo by Lyndon Fox.

Like my other contacts, the O'Brien family knew nothing of my bike. I had spoken with several former team members, nonetheless, and I knew that #49 was a team bike and that the water-cooled bike in the Harley-Davidson museum had a similar serial number. I still had no idea how the bike made it to Missouri, but I had enough proof to move forward with the preservation. The team members and I were not getting any younger, and if my timing was right, we were approaching the 40th anniversary of the last year the Harley-Davidson MX team existed, so I had a goal for when I wanted to get this preservation completed.

At this time, the only other riders for the team that I could not get in contact with were Marty Tripes—more on Marty later—and Rich Eierstedt. Rich passed away back in 2010; he had joined the team late in the 1977 season, just in time for the Trans-AMA series. Rest in peace, Rich.

Marty was #558 for the 1977 team, but was #38 when this picture was taken at the 1977 Olympiad. Note the dirt track tires and mechanic Don Habermehl in the background. Photo by Mark Kiel.

Rich was #11 for the 1977 team. This photo was taken at the Rabbit Run Trans-AMA in Plano, Texas. Photo by Joseph Savant.

I placed the #49 up on my trusty Harbor Freight motorcycle lift and started assessing the plan. So far, I treated my research as if I was a detective, and I would treat this tear-down no differently. I would inspect each part for clues and run any questions I had past the team members. It would be like an episode of *CSI*, only with motorcycle parts....

CHAPTER 5

THE PRESERVATION BEGINS

Gas Tank and Seat

It was January 2017, and the first parts to come off #49 were the gas tank and seat: nothing out of the ordinary there. The seat had the HOSS orange plastic seat base and the foam was still in good shape, but the cover was torn in the back along a seam. The cover was also riveted on, not glued or stapled.

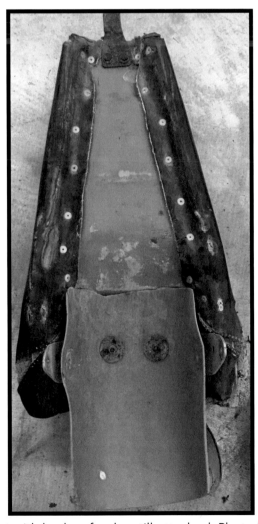

Underside of seat with broken fender still attached. Photo by Keith Geisner.

The tank was modified with a right-hand side petcock and fork reliefs. I had observed two petcock styles during my research: a ball valve with lever style and a Pingel Motorsport Inc. petcock. The decals were covered and protected with the addition of clear vinyl. (I had noted this on several other team bikes during my research.) The fuel cap had a brazed-on hook—I guessed this was to tether the cap to the tank so that it would not get lost. This hook was also visible on several other team bike photos found on the internet. These parts were placed right behind my stand on a shelf, where they would stay until they would be cleaned and reinstalled months later.

Fork reliefs were added for clearance and fuel cap hook added
to possibly tether to bike. Photo by Keith Geisner.

See outline of the clear vinyl over the tank
decal and also the right-hand-mounted
petcock. Photo by Keith Geisner.

The water-cooled MX250 has a Pingel
Motorsport Inc. petcock. Photo by Mark Wick.

Next, I removed the fenders and side number plates. The rear fender, as noted in my original photos, was broken. The rear fender was bolted to the rear seat and to the rear frame. For quick removal, the seat and rear fender came off with only two bolts as an assembly. This made sense for an MX race bike. The rear fender was from HOSS and the color was orange. Since the fender was unusable, this item went on my list of parts to research and locate. The front fender was also a HOSS, a "duckbill" design where the front of the fender is flared to help keep debris from the front tire away from the rider. There were no clues on the fender, and I could not determine if it had ever had any decals. Luckily, the bike had been stored out of the sun and the plastic wasn't faded. The front fender was in great shape, so I placed it on the shelf to await clean-up.

HOSS duckbill front fender. Photo by Keith Geisner.

When I removed the side number plates, the bike was on my lift, so I was looking at it from a different angle. I could see up behind the side number plates and the back side of the airbox. At this time, something caught my eye: on the inside of the number plates, I noted rub marks caused by the rear shocks, but the rear shocks currently on the bike did not touch these same areas. I knew right away that those marks had been caused by Fox air shocks, the same brand used by the team. This was an encouraging find, as it indicated that the shocks currently on the bike were put on at a later time and, in turn, hinted that the bike was tied to the Harley-Davidson MX race team.

Side number plates removed, exposing Fox shock rub marks
behind the #4 and #9. Photo by Keith Geisner.

Another thing I noted was that the side number plates had two sets of mounting holes, close to one another, which told me these side plates could have been on a different frame at one time. The side number plates were secured with DZUS fasteners, commonly found on C&J frames.

Next was the front number plate. The plate was typical of the times, but what stood out was the number plate bracket. The bracket was a gray plastic that was riveted to the number plate, and each end was formed around the fork tubes. The plastic was flexible enough to allow you to remove and easily replace the number plate, yet strong enough to grip the fork tubes and not allow it to come off during a race. I began reviewing the team pics on the internet and found that they had all used this type of front number plate mount. I had never seen this type of bracket before and I would later reach out to several plastics manufacturers to correctly ID the plastic used for it.

Finally, I got around to the airbox, which couldn't be taken out without removing all the previous items. To replace the air filter, one had to remove the back panel of the airbox, which faced the rear tire. It fit tightly inside the frame and was mounted by three fasteners. I was nervous as I removed it because I had to manipulate it carefully for it to come out without sustaining any damage. Fortunately, the plastic was tough and flexible. The airbox had a couple of different mounting holes drilled in it as well, same as the number plates. I reached out to Don Habermehl to ask about the extra mounting holes and he said it was very common to swap number plates and parts between bikes.

It's pertinent at this point to talk a little about HOSS Plastics. HOSS was located in Linndale, Ohio, and specialized in rotational molding. They were an aftermarket company that made replacement motorcycle plastic parts. All the plastic on the H-D team bikes was manufactured by HOSS.

According to Wikipedia, "Rotational Molding involves a heated hollow mold which is filled with a charge or shot weight of material. It is then slowly rotated (usually around two perpendicular axes), causing the softened material to disperse and stick to the walls of the mold. In order to maintain even thickness throughout the part, the mold continues to rotate at all times during the heating phase and to avoid sagging or deformation also during the cooling phase."

I discussed HOSS and their processes with both Tom Volin and Don Habermehl. Both had the opportunity to tour the facility and witness the molding process. According to them, the owner made motorcycle plastic to pay for his hobbies. He had his own kiln and poured his own aluminum molds that measured roughly 8'x8'. One mold would do a whole set of plastics for a bike. The mold would spin like a gyroscope through the heating and cooling processes.

Handlebars and Levers

Now that the fenders, number plates, seat, and gas tank were removed from the bike, I turned my attention to the handlebars. The bars matched what the team would have used, but I questioned the levers, perches, and throttle. The grips were a diamond-pattern grip and I was able to find them on eBay. At this stage of the preservation I believed that the team used Oury grips, but I'm sure it was the rider's preference. The clutch lever and perch were stock production Harley-Davidson MX, so I knew they were not team originals.

The throttle assembly was an Amal brand. I believed the team had used Gasser Gunner, which I found on eBay. The front brake and perch were Magura. After learning this, I reached out to Don, and he confirmed that all team bikes used Magura lever assemblies. Now I was certain the handlebars and front brake lever assembly were of team origin. The non-race team controls were added later, and the correct controls would be easy to source.

Motor

While the bike was still standing on its two wheels, the next item to come off was the motor. I first unbolted the Moto Plat coil from the frame. This ignition was correct for the bike, since by 1978 the team had switched to Moto Plat ignition from Dansi, which was used on the 1975 to early 1977 team bikes. The motor was unremarkable for the most part. I noted the production rear upper motor mount brackets, which were out of place since the C&J frame tubing was a different diameter than the production frame. The mounts could not tighten down fully, leaving a gap between the brackets.

Other items of note included the giant snap ring on the clutch basket, which was safety-wired, and there were punch marks on the clutch inner hub nut and drive gear nut. The punch marks were done as a locking device to keep the nut from backing off. I sent photos to Tom Volin and Don Habermehl and asked if these three items were some of their workmanship, to which they replied they were not. This was further proof that the motor was not a team motor. After removing all the motor mount bolts, the motor simply pulled out, leaving a bare rolling frame in its path.

Suspension and Wheels

Next on the list was to strip the frame of its legs. I started with removing the foot pegs and rear brake lever. The rear brake lever was handmade—even the foldable end of the brake had welded-on nubs to keep your foot from slipping off. The foldable lever was a Penton Hi-Point product that was welded on. The product is a gear-shift lever that had been flipped over and used as the brake. I noted a similar foot brake lever in a picture of one of Rex Staten's #31 bikes, so this confirmed it was a team-made part. Tom Volin also confirmed this in a telephone conversation, in which he told me he had made a few of those rear brake pedals. This rear brake design was carried over from Tom's days with Husqvarna.

Custom-made rear foot brake lever with foldable end. Photo by Keith Geisner.

At this point, I did a deep dive into studying the rear brake pedals used on the C&J-framed bikes the team used. I noticed a total of three different configurations. One was like mine, where you had a foot brake lever that actuated the rear brake arm using a metal rod. The second type used a different-style foot lever with a cable attached to it from the rear, similar to a Honda CR setup. The cable then went through a hole in the frame and back to the rear brake arm, where it slid into a bracket on the rear brake plate and then was attached to the brake arm.

The water-cooled MX250 has the second type of brake configuration with the brake cable routed through the frame. Photo by Mark Wick.

The third rear brake setup was similar to the second, but the cable was mounted in the middle of the foot brake lever, similar to the production H-D MX250 setup. The cable was then routed *inside* the frame, not through, and over the swingarm where it was mounted to a bracket on the rear brake plate and then secured to the brake lever.

The third brake configuration, as seen on this 1976 bike. Photo by John Brier.

The discovery of the three different rear brake configurations helped me identify my next clues. As I removed the rear wheel, something on the brake plate caught my attention. The rear wheel was from a Yamaha YZ and so was the rear brake plate, but what I saw next I knew wasn't Yamaha YZ. There were two things on the rear brake plate that were not from stock: bearings and a sleeve that were machined into the axle hole of the brake plate. The stock YZ brake plate used a bushing only, but this brake plate was machined out on both sides and fitted with two bearings and a sleeve; also, there was a little bracket with a hole welded to the brake plate. This small bracket that appeared to have broken off at one time had to have been for a cable-actuated rear brake. This told me that the rear brake plate had to have been on another team bike that used a cable-actuated rear brake configuration.

Rear brake backing plate modified with brake cable bracket and
outer/inner axle bearing. Photo by Keith Geisner.

As I moved forward with the disassembly, the shocks were next. They came off easily, with no additional clues to note other than that they were stock production Harley-Davidson MX250 shocks. I also noticed the rear axle adjusters were custom-made. I sent photos to Don and Tom and they both confirmed these parts were made in the race department. The rear wheel was stock YZ, and I noted that orange zip-ties were used to support the spokes where they crossed. I had previously noticed in museum photos the use of zip-ties on the water-cooled MX bike, so I was careful not to knock any off. The only thing remaining on the rear of the bike was the swingarm. I elected to tackle that last and moved on to the triples, forks, and front wheel. As I removed the front wheel, I observed that all fasteners that were holding anything to the frame or triple clamps were standard thread, and that the only thing metric was what held on the wheels and some Allen bolts on the motor. The front wheel and forks came off with little effort, with nothing to note other than they were Yamaha YZ. As I removed the triple clamps, I noted they used Timken bearings in the steering stem. I cleaned up the triples and sent photos to the team for feedback. Don replied that they were made by the race department. Lastly, the front and rear rims were stock Yamaha YZ, and I observed that all the team bikes used SUN aftermarket rims. These could still be easily sourced and updated later.

Race department triple trees. Notice the wear marks from the number plate. Photo by Keith Geisner.

One final thing I noticed was a little notch machined out around the lower right-hand triple clamp bolt. I pointed this out to the team, and all replied that it was machined out for a front brake cable guide. This was interesting information, because my bike had a left-hand cable-actuated front wheel, which told me that the triple trees on #49 could have been on a different bike, or that the bike at one time used a front wheel and forks that had a right-hand brake on the wheel.

Notch added for front brake cable guide. Photo by Keith Geisner.

I then reviewed pictures of the team and noticed that Marty Tripes used a front wheel with a right-hand brake on some of his bikes. So, I had a bare frame—swingarm still attached—and I was finding parts on the bike that could have been from other team bikes. This only added to #49's mystery.

Marty Tripes 1977 Winter-AMA. Notice his bike has the right-hand front brake cable routing. Photo by Lyndon Fox.

I sent an email to the team, asking about the random parts on my bike and where they thought my bike stood with the team. Clyde Denzer replied, "Sounds like you are moving forward with your restoration. We never had back-up bikes. I do not recall having extra frames stacked up anywhere, but it makes sense that a batch of frames would have been made at one time. The team mechanics/mechanic had to keep one bike going for his rider. A severe crash would have been the end of the day for that rider. There was only one point in the MX program that we had 3 riders. That was when we also had a large transporter with drivers/mechanics. Tom Volin and Don Habermehl were the main men then. You can be certain your bike had different shocks at the beginning of its life."

Don Habermehl also replied: "Parts did not always stay with a particular bike. Wheels and just about all pieces got switched around. I'll bet some time or another number plates got moved from one bike to another. I would guess that this was a later frame with Yamaha wheels and brakes because I'm sure Don Kudalski was the last to ride for us. Tom Volin was the last mechanic to be in the field. I did some work on the motors but for the most part I switched to working on the flat-track equipment and battle of the twins bike and motors. Good Luck, Don."

Frame

As stated earlier, the frame on #49 was made by Jeff Cole at C&J. Jeff had estimated he made anywhere from six to ten frames for the team. The team switched to these frames around the 1977 USGP time frame and used them through 1978. One could determine when the switch occurred because the rear frame loop was deleted, and they had quickly switched over to the Cross Up swingarm and Fox air-shocks. A few months after this change, the team had three riders: Rex Staten (#31), Marty Tripes (#558), and Rich Eierstedt (#11) going into the Trans-AMA series.

1977 USGP, the team started the switch to C&J frames #32 and Fox shocks #31. Photo by Phil Davy.

Swingarm

Patience was always key during the preservation, and that was exactly what it took to remove the swingarm from the frame. The swingarm bolt was a threaded shaft that was hollow, with nuts on each end, similar to what one would find on a Husqvarna dirt bike. Both nuts came loose with minimal effort, but the shaft was not so easy.

After several days of soaking the shaft with penetrating oil, heating and cooling, with no luck, I finally got creative. I got some all-thread and a large socket. Similar to the way one would remove a stubborn piston pin, I ran the all-thread through the center of the swingarm bolt and applied force by tightening the nut on the all-thread. With force applied, I began tapping with a hammer and finally saw movement. After I had tapped it back and forth a couple of times, the swingarm bolt came out. It was a joyous moment. The hang-up was that the swingarm bolt went through an aluminum sleeve inside the swingarm. Dissimilar metals never play well together. During the week that I struggled with the swingarm bolt, I came up with a cool photograph idea. When the swingarm was finally removed, I put down some cardboard on the floor of my shop and began to lay out the entire bike in pieces. I used a twelve-foot step ladder and took a photo from the top, capturing the entire layout of the parts. It was a great shot of a disassembled factory H-D MX.

#49 awaiting clean-up. Photo by Keith Geisner.

Every time I learned something about the bike or reached a milestone such as the removal of the swingarm, I would send photos and stories to the team members. I also posted updated photos on the Harley-Davidson MX Owners Facebook page. I loved getting feedback and at the same time hoped for new information about #49. There had yet to be any hits on the serial number on the frame or on how the bike made it to Missouri.

Now that the bike was disassembled, it was time to clean, inspect and reassemble. The only things I planned to replace were the tubes, bearings, seals, gaskets and anything that wasn't installed by the race department. To begin this next phase, I cleaned my Harbor Freight bike lift, reorganized my tools, swept the shop floor, and broke out the shop rags and other cleaning supplies.

At this stage of the preservation, it dawned on me that 2018 would be the 40th anniversary of the Harley-Davidson MX team. I instantly became anxious. Who else was aware of this? Would there be a celebration?

I reached out to the director of events at the Harley-Davidson Museum in Milwaukee. I explained the forty-year mark and offered some suggestions of what they might do. I suggested getting the surviving team members together and shared their contact information. The director informed me that 2018 was already booked up for the 115-year anniversary of the company and that there was little chance any other events would be planned. She agreed nonetheless to take my idea to the board.

I sent a follow-up email within a week, only to learn there would be no planned activities related to the MX team's history. I was told to stay in touch after I completed the restoration and that perhaps they could work out a visit. I set my goal to have the bike completed by 2018.

I also reached out to the AMA Museum to see if the 40th anniversary of the Harley-Davidson MX team might be mentioned in their magazine, but there were no plans. The person with whom I spoke thought it was a great idea, however, and this added to my sense of purpose in completing the preservation and sharing the team's history.

Reassembly

I began with the frame. It was the foundation of the project that all other parts would eventually join. The goal was to remove all the years of dirt and grime, while protecting the original paint. It required hand-rubbing with polishing compound to remove any fading/oxidation and bring back the color. This took time and patience.

While engaged in this process I kept my eyes out for more clues. I saw that the exhaust mount had broken off at some point and had been reattached roughly ¼" from its original location. I also noted that the left-hand large gusset that attached the down tube to the back-bone tube had a stress crack. This indicated that the bike had some hours on it and had been ridden hard. I also discovered the frame had been repainted at intervals, noting several layers of paint. If the exhaust mount repair was performed at a race, that might have been the frame's last race since it wasn't repainted.

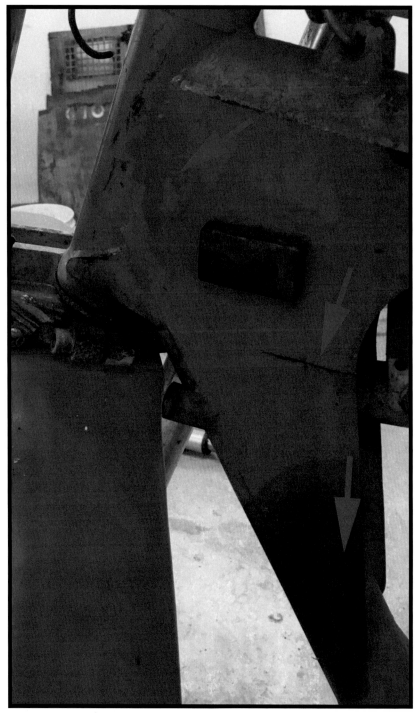

Note the multiple layers of paint, horizontal crack in the frame gusset and repaired exhaust bracket. Heat from the weld discolored the frame paint. Photo by Keith Geisner.

Next my focus was on the triple trees. I confirmed with Don Habermehl that they were made by the Harley-Davidson race department. As referenced earlier, there was a small, machined-out relief for the right-hand front brake cable guide. The steering-head bearings were Timken bearings, so they would be easy to source.

I took the original fasteners and cleaned them up non-abrasively so as not to remove any identification marks. The handlebar mounts had extra holes for adjustability. The only other thing that caught my attention was a slight wear mark in the lower triple from the front number plate rubbing against it, which also indicated a lot of ride-time. Once the triple trees were reinstalled with freshly greased new bearings, I turned my attention to the swingarm.

The swingarm was made by Cross Up. Besides new swingarm bushings, there wasn't anything else I needed to do but clean it up. I did not want to go with a shiny finish because I was doing a preservation, not a restoration or show bike. It had to look like it did back in the day after being washed from a day of racing. So, instead of hitting it hard with compound and a buffer, I simply cleaned it up and used some finesse compound to remove any oxidation. I was careful of the two Dunlop stickers on either side. I had seen these same decals on another team bike owned by Menalco Solis III. It was important not to damage these during clean-up.

The swingarm bearings were difficult to source. I made inquiries on many Facebook group pages, but came up empty. The bushings that came with the bike were a fiber type that someone on Facebook referred to as Swenco top hat bushings. I was surprised, as I would have thought that needle-bearing or bronze bushings would have been used. Fortunately, I had recently acquired a box of motorcycle parts that contained a new set of bronze Yamaha XS650 swingarm bearings. They were the right length and inside diameter, so all I had to do was turn down the outer diameter. This worked well and was an upgrade to the original bearings.

With the swingarm cleaned, the decals preserved, and fresh bronze bushings installed, the swingarm was ready to be reinstalled. The swingarm bolt and nuts already had a little rust on them, and I was afraid to get them re-plated as they would look too new. I also feared losing these pieces at the plating company. I simply bead-blasted them and then applied a clear coat to protect against further rust. If this ever became an issue, these parts could be easily removed and re-plated. With the swingarm installed, #49 was starting to look like a motocross bike again.

Close up of #558 Marty Tripes Fox shocks and Cross Up swingarm. Also note
Trelleborg rear tire and 59-tooth rear sprocket. Photo by Lyndon Fox.

Next, I turned my attention to the suspension. I sourced and located on eBay a set of rear Fox shocks with the correct date code from when the team would have used them. Surprisingly, when they showed up there was actually a touch of orange paint on and around the mount area—the same color as the frame. Coincidence?

Next, I disassembled the front forks. The front forks were Yamaha YZ forks from the right time period. I read an article in *Cycle News* that stated Rex Staten ran the stock YZ forks on his bike. Nothing out of the ordinary there. They were quite dirty on the inside, but with a little cleaning, new seals, and oil they were ready to go. With the suspension accounted for and installed, it was now time to focus on the wheels.

The wheels were from a Yamaha YZ as well. I took great care in removing the tires to not damage the rims. I used rim protectors and had few problems in removing them. The color of the rim bands threw me for a loop! They were orange and pink! After posting photos of these on the Harley-Davidson MX250 Owners Facebook page, I learned that they were H-D rim bands that were also used on the production version in 1978.

Next, I wanted to investigate whether the tires were from the Harley-Davidson race department or if they had been replaced after the bike's time with the team. The rear tire was a Dunlop K88 with a date code of 146 and location code of ET. The front tire was an IRC, a brand I doubted the team would have used, so I focused first on the Dunlop.

Could the date code have indicated the fourteenth week of 1976 or 1986? I reached out to Dunlop Consumer Affairs and got an answer within a week. The email read: "The tire was made at Kobe factory. ET means Kobe factory. The Kobe factory was destroyed by an earthquake in January 1995. So, the tire was made in the week of 14, 1986, K88 was very popular in the 80s."

This confirmed that the tires on the bike did not come from the Harley-Davidson team and were replaced sometime later. I had the green light to replace them. Since the swingarm bore Dunlop decals, I elected to use Dunlop tires. With the wheels cleaned and new tubes and tires installed, things were looking pretty good. It was time to move on to fitting the new brakes and sourcing a rear sprocket.

Brakes were easy to source, since they were from a 1977 Yamaha YZ. The rear sprocket was another matter. I couldn't just buy any 1977 YZ sprocket—I had to source the same style the team used. The sprocket that came with the bike was a solid aluminum 59T rear sprocket. Mechanic Don Habermehl confirmed the tooth count. He said that, depending on the track, they would either run a 58 or 59 rear sprocket. I noticed that Rex Staten ran a few bikes with a solid rear sprocket, but most of the team bikes had lightening holes. Since that was what Kudalski ran, I had to run the same thing. Fortunately, there were a few sprocket makers out there that could make anything. After the front and rear wheels were completed and installed, I had a rolling chassis.

The preservation process was into March 2017 and there were hard-to-find pieces that weighed on me. One was the rear fender and the other was a team cylinder head that Kudalski ran. HOSS made the rear fender, but they had made them for other models as well: same shape but different colors. I sourced a HOSS rear fender for a Honda that I was willing to go to extremes to make work. As for the head, Cagiva MXRs and RX250s used a similar head—if I had to go to extremes with one of those, I would as well. The Cagiva head was a later version of the same head Kudalski used in 1978. The search was on and I posted alerts to several flat-track Facebook groups. I received a few leads, but they were all dead ends.

While the searches for the head and rear fender continued, I turned to the seat that still had the original team seat cover. It was torn on the rear corner and I had to get it fixed. The foam still felt great. The seat had to go back just the way the team would have made it.

The cover was riveted onto a plastic base made by HOSS. I carefully removed the cover and measured the rivets. With the seat all apart, I cleaned up and replaced the seat mount nut plates. They were rusty and needed help. With the rivet dimensions recorded, I was able to source identical rivets. I got lucky and found a local upholsterer who did motorcycle seats for the best motorcycle restorer in the area, Jeff Weier, so I knew I couldn't go wrong. He matched up the material perfectly. I gave him the old seat cover so he could work from the same patterns, plus photos of the team bikes from back in the day. After a few weeks the seat was complete, and I could not have been happier with the result. With the seat out of the way, I could now focus on the next item.

The seat was disassembled, rivets measured and hardware replaced. Photo by Keith Geisner.

I unstuck the motor the day I brought it home. Before I try to break any motor free, I remove the head and intake. This was no exception. I then soak the top of the piston and crank housing with penetrating oil, letting it sit for a day or two. Then I would remove the flywheel cover and secure a special tool to the flywheel to use as leverage. I had always had success with this method.

This motor did not take much to free it up. That told me it was locked up from sitting and it didn't take an early retirement from a seized top or bottom end. The tricky thing about Aermacchi MX250s, I discovered, is that they used acorn-style nuts to secure the cylinder to studs coming up out of the cases. These nuts were located a couple of inches down into the cylinder. Dirt and debris liked to collect in this area, making it difficult to secure a socket to the nut. It turned out that I could not get any of these nuts to break free. That meant I had to take a drill and drill from the top down until I hit a stud. To make sure I drilled dead center of the nuts, I had a buddy make me a drill guide. This is a tube-type tool that my drill bit goes through and holds it perfectly center as I drilled down. The drill guide worked like a charm. Once I got the cylinder free from the cases, I was delighted to find the crank in great shape. The cranks for the MX250s were one of the hardest parts to find.

Now that the cylinder was off, I turned my attention to the flywheel. I bought a Moto Plat flywheel puller on eBay. One thing I have learned with taking motors apart is that if you use the right tool, it made the experience so much more enjoyable. Parts are not destroyed, and it takes way less effort.

The flywheel and stator came off without any problems. I then turned the motor around and started removing the clutch cover and all the parts behind it, which included the clutch assembly, drive gear, shift mechanism, and shift shaft. The cases were now ready to split. (Before I get into the case-splitting segment, remember that every assembly and piece I removed was bagged and tagged. Also, I had recently purchased a case-splitting tool and used it on my nephew's Yamaha race bike. These case splitters are worth every penny—no hammering, just secure and tighten. The cases come apart with ease and no beating or prying with screwdrivers is necessary).

Now that the cases were apart, I kept the gear cluster together and placed the assembly into a large plastic bag. The shift barrel came out next, followed by the crank. I inspected everything before bagging it, in case any replacements needed to be ordered. The motor was completely disassembled, and it was time for a break.

Rear Fender

As I mentioned earlier, the rear fender on my bike was broken off. HOSS had been the plastic manufacturer for the H-D race bikes; they also made the same style of fenders for other MX models as well—in different colors. I ran across a NOS rear HOSS fender for a Honda CR. It was what I needed, but it was the wrong color. I had just finished making a plaster mold of the rear fender for a reproduction when I received a message from Menalco Solis: he needed a few parts to complete his team bike and some of those parts I could replicate from parts on #49. Menalco had an extra rear fender from the team that had come with his bike. The fender even had "Killer" written on it! It was meant for my bike!

Menalco was willing to trade me the rear fender and a team tank strap for the missing parts he needed. I could not pass up this opportunity and I readily agreed to the trade. We were working together to preserve Harley-Davidson MX team history. When the fender arrived, I was in heaven! I never dreamed I would find an original team rear fender for the bike. It was like finding a needle in a haystack. I had another idea for a photo as well.

The rear fender joins the rest of the team panels after forty years. Photo by Keith Geisner.

The search for a head was really weighing on me. As I stated before, Cagiva used a later version of the head Kudalski raced with during the 1978 season. I got a wild idea and started searching for Cagiva heads on Facebook. I joined all the Cagiva dirt bike groups I could, requesting one of these heads. Finally, I got a break: a seller in Greece posted a Cagiva RX250 rod kit. It was the same rod the MX250 used. It was priced right, and I bought it without hesitation. That night, the same seller posted another RX250 rod kit and I bought that one as well. These were extremely rare parts in the U.S.

I emailed the seller and asked what other RX parts he might have and if he had a head. He replied that he had no other parts, but that he did have a friend with a head. A week later we struck a deal and the head was on its way. I was super-stoked!

Newly received rod kits and Cagiva head. Photo by Keith Geisner.

Another person I had contacted for a cylinder head was an administrator of one of the Cagiva Facebook groups I had joined, Manfred Wurth. Manfred returned a message I sent him, and we started communicating. He had a Cagiva head as well, and within a week we struck a deal. Within a few weeks my second Cagiva head showed up and, to my surprise, he sent me a T-shirt from his motorcycle club. I thanked him for the gift.

By now I'm sure readers are wondering what I was going to do with those Cagiva heads. They were a later version of the head used by Kudalski in '78, so the cylinder head DNA was there. The heads had begun as full radial heads, which meant the head was cast and both sides had full-supported fins that were symmetrical. The heads were made at the Aermacchi plant in Italy. If Harley-Davidson had kept the MX program alive, the heads might have come out on the 1979 production models. Of course, this didn't happen. I confirmed this with lead mechanic Tom Volin, who when I asked replied, "You mean the production head."

When Harley-Davidson sold out to Cagiva, naturally the new Cagiva MX bikes used this head. The only difference was that the molds were modified to remove some of the fins on the right-hand side of the head to make room for the right-hand-exiting exhaust. This was the opposite of the head changes on Kudalski's bike. Since his bike had a left-hand-exiting exhaust, his heads had to have the left-hand fins trimmed down for clearance. These early production heads were also popular on the Harley-Davidson flat-track bikes.

Since I now had a Cagiva head, I had the perfect platform to make the head I needed that would resemble the head Kudalski used—just to get me by until a real head could be sourced. I basically had to add back the fins that were removed from the right side of the Cagiva head. How would I do this? The heads were aluminum and the fins area 1/8" thick, so with some 1/8" flat stock and a good TIG welder, I was in business. Luckily for me, my brother worked in an aluminum casting plant where aluminum was plentiful and TIG welders were easy to find, but I had to put in some elbow grease first.

I had to copy the fins on the left-hand side of the head and make patterns to use to cut the new fins out of the flat stock I had. Once the fin patterns were cut out, there was still a lot of massaging to do to make everything fit perfectly. I then had to tape everything in place, so my brother knew how everything went together. All the pieces had to be welded in order. If one piece was welded out of sequence, it could possibly ruin the entire head. I told my brother I was in no hurry and that he had a few months to get it done. About twice a week, he would send me updated pictures of the progress. He would even send me videos of the fins getting TIG-welded on. When the final project was complete, I could not believe my eyes: it was as if I was holding Harley-Davidson history in my hands. There was still some massaging to do, but I could see light at the end of the tunnel. I geared up for the push to the finish line.

Finished radial head ready for assembly. Photo by Keith Geisner.

I was still able to find any piece I needed for the motor. I purchased a new Moto Plat ignition, new clutch plates, a bearing kit for the lower end along with the seals, and a gasket kit. I took a day off work just so I could concentrate and get the motor back together.

The motor is ready for assembly. Photo by Keith Geisner.

While I was cleaning up the motor cases, the factory paint came off easily—and I didn't intend for that to happen. I elected to clean them up and repaint them. Now the motor cases would match the new top end assembly I had purchased. The shifter the team had used was a modified shifter lever from a stock MX and a foldable shifter sold by Hi-Point, same as the foot brake lever. Hi-Point offered shifters that were just a shaft with a foldable toe-piece that you had to weld onto the existing shifter. By the end of the day, I had the whole motor reassembled except for the head. With the motor assembled, I placed it in the frame. That reminded me that I still needed rear upper motor mounts.

I reached out to Don Habermehl to see what the team had used. He replied that the team made their own mounts in the race department and that they were made out of steel, since they had issues with aluminum ones breaking. Don went on to say that he made the rubber air-cleaner boots from scratch, using Devcon soft rubber. The swingarm chain guide was also made from scratch. I searched all the photos of these brackets I could find to try to get an idea of the design. In the end, I made my own design and sent it to my brother to make out of aluminum. If the team bikes' mounts were handmade, mine would be as well. I could have made a set of steel mounts, but the bike would not be ridden so aluminum would be just fine.

Rubber chain guide handmade by Don Habermehl. Photo by Keith Geisner.

Silencer

The remainder of the bike required only some elbow grease and attention. The silencer was missing, but when I examined Kudalski's photo and the ones of the water-cooled museum bike, they appeared to have used J&R brand silencers. Tom Volin also confirmed this. I was lucky enough to already have one in my possession.

The only thing I had to do was make a silencer bracket that resembled the one on Kudalski's bike and the water-cooled bike, since they both used the same silencer. Working from pictures I had of both bikes,

I could tell they had similar brackets welded to them. I aimed for a bracket style in between the two, and it turned out great. Since the pipe had a lot of surface rust but was still reasonably solid, I decided to bead-blast and paint it. I then test-fitted it to the motor with the head in place to determine what fins needed to be trimmed on the head to allow clearance. Trimming the fins of the head was not an easy task—in fact, it was nerve-wracking because a lot of work had already gone into the head. Now I was trimming it. Once I finished, though, the pipe fit great and the bike was starting to look complete.

Airbox

I really lucked out in that the airbox was complete. The airbox was made by HOSS and it came with the back-access cover in place, the filter cage, and the securing rod. All these items cleaned up very well. The plastic was only slightly faded and a quick scrubbing with soapy water made it look like new. I made a filter from scratch because I did not know where to begin to look for one. Once it was completed, I set the airbox back in the frame—it was a tight fit. I got to thinking this airbox could have been used as early as 1976. It had extra mounting holes drilled in it, so I knew for sure it was in a different frame at one time. I believed the team used Champion frames in 1976 and early 1977. I knew it was not made specifically for the C&J frame, but was a very similar design indeed.

The airbox was completely disassembled and cleaned. Note the multiple mounting holes. Photo by Keith Geisner.

With the airbox in place, I cleaned up the carburetor boot. This boot was handmade by Don Habermehl. According to Don, he made clay molds of what the boots should look like, and then mixed rubber Devcon to make rubber boots, one at a time. He did the same thing for the swingarm guard and some gas tank supports. These molds weren't always perfect, so he had to do some whittling to make them just right. Knowing this made me feel lucky this bike still had these rare, one-off pieces that would have been impossible to find.

With the carb thoroughly cleaned, I mounted the carb and snugged everything down. I purchased a new throttle and clutch cable, since the ones that were on the bike were not usable. With the handlebars repainted and the controls in place, the bike was looking great. It was time for the plastic and the gas tank.

As in the case of the airbox, the fenders and number plates cleaned up easily. There was little sun fade thanks to the bike being stored out of direct sunlight. As I mentioned previously, the rear fender had been mounted to the seat. With the fender firmly reattached to the seat, I placed it on the bike and secured it. The front fender was just as easy, followed by the side number plates. I took care not to damage or remove any of the side numbers or their protective clear vinyl overlay. The same went for the gas tank. I used finesse compound and hand-rubbed the entire tank to bring the color back, followed by some wax. With the tank in place, I secured it with the race-team gas tank strap that I had received from Menalco. The bike was about 90 percent complete, but there were a few more details that needed to be addressed.

Gas tank mounted and team gas tank strap in place. Photo by Keith Geisner.

One detail was the front brake cable guide that attached to the front fender. I reviewed several pictures of the 1977-78 team bikes and studied this little guide, trying to determine the source. I blew up photos and shared them with the team. The best response I got was from John Ingham, who said it looked like a cable clamp they had likely sourced from a local hardware store. I searched several hardware stores, from large chain stores to small retailers, and could find no similar clamp. I had enough good photos of it that I could picture what it would look like in my hands. As fate would have it, like many occurrences during this preservation, I had recently acquired a 1976 Husqvarna WR360. This wasn't just any Husky WR360, but one that was raced at the 1976 International Six Day Trials (ISDT) in Austria by a fellow Missourian, Jim Simmons. Jim won a silver medal that year. It was strange that, now that I was coming to the end of the Harley-Davidson MX team bike preservation, I came into possession of another motorcycle of historical significance.

Jim Simmons and I with his 1976 ISDT Silver Medal Husqvarna. Jim was a four-time ISDT qualifier and medaled three times. Photo by Keith Geisner.

These Husqvarna motorcycles used a special rubber bracket that secured the rear fender and airbox to the frame. These brackets looked exactly like the front brake cable guide I had pictured in my head. I couldn't believe it! I had been thinking about the guide for two or three weeks, all while walking right by them in my own shop the whole time!

Tom Volin was very familiar with Husqvarna and this all made sense to him. He had raced for Husqvarna in the late '60s and early '70s. Tom carried over the rear brake lever design from Husqvarna and implemented it onto the H-D MX bikes. It made sense that this was the front brake cable guide that the team could have used.

Front brake cable guide. Photo by Keith Geisner.

With the front brake cable guide mounted onto the fender, I focused my attention on the second detail I had noticed last-minute: my mag cover looked a little different from the other covers I had observed on the team bikes. It looked like the team bike mag covers had some material removed that would have covered the front sprocket. After examining several photos, I concluded that all of the covers had this modification.

I was certain it was for easy access to the front sprocket and to keep mud from getting packed in behind it. This would be an easy modification for me to make.

I had been thinking of how I was going to display the bike. I didn't want people touching it, so I took a page out of my father's playbook. My father had restored cars throughout his life, and his first major show car was a 1956 Chevy. Dad was a master of auto restoration and customization. When he showed his '56, he made a set of barrier stands from scratch. He had a total of six stands that were painted gold to match the gold metal flake in the car's paint. With this in mind, I began searching the internet for barrier stands. I found a set of four that were very close to Harley-Davidson orange and ordered them. To add some personal touches, I ordered some classic Harley-Davidson #1 patches from eBay and glued them to each stand. This really made them pop.

Around this time, my brother Jeff called me and asked if I knew where Dad's '56 barrier stands were. We narrowed it down to a friend of Dad's to whom he had loaned the barriers in the '80s. I reached out to Dad's friend and sure enough, he still had them. I picked them up and we surprised Dad for his birthday.

The second part of displaying the bike was making a bike stand similar to what the team used. These were wooden boxes that were painted black and had an orange stripe on each side with the Harley-Davidson MX script inside the orange stripe. When I asked Don Habermehl about the bike stands, he told me how they came about. The team was at a dealership in California and they needed bike stands, so the dealership provided the material. They made a total of four boxes, each one slightly smaller than the next. They did this so they could stack the boxes on top of each other and they would take up less room in the race truck, like Russian Matryoshka dolls. With the story fresh in my mind, I set out to make my own bike stand. I looked at several pictures and scaled it accordingly. The finished product almost fooled Don. He said that if it didn't look so shiny, he would have had a hard time telling if it was an original or not.

Finished bike stand with decals applied. Photo by Keith Geisner.

Not only did I plan out the barrier stands to show the bike, I also sourced an MX jersey maker who could replicate the jersey the 1977-78 Harley-Davidson MX team would have worn. The idea of a cool picture came to mind, just like the exploded view I took after I had the bike disassembled. I had some jerseys made to display with the bike. With the jerseys and stands in hand, I cleaned up a section of my shop. The back of my overhead doors made a good backdrop for pictures, plus it allowed me to hang the jerseys above the bike. I placed two of the barrier stands in front of the bike and strung the orange plastic chain between them. I couldn't imagine it looking any cooler: there it was, the bike sitting on a replica team bike stand, with team members' jerseys hanging in the background. I had been updating people on this bike for over a year on Facebook, so I wanted to take pictures of the finished product that would take their breath away. I took several pictures from the front, back, and sides. I also set up my twelve-foot step ladder to take an overhead shot. The results and feedback I received were exactly what I was hoping for.

Finally finished with #49. Photo by Keith Geisner.

CHAPTER 6

A BREAK IN THE SERIAL NUMBER

The frame serial number was still a mystery and I had the idea to send a note to my contact at the H-D museum. I took a picture of my frame number and the blurry view of the water-cooled frame number and asked them if the museum's bike had a serial number similar to mine. About a week went by before my museum contact got back to me. Though the archives department determined that the serial numbers were similar, he could not give me the number off the water-cooled bike for privacy reasons. I was okay with that response; as long as the numbers were similar, that connected my bike with the factory MX team. Knowing what the serial number meant would be even better.

Right-side view of the water-cooled team bike located in the
Harley-Davidson museum. Photo by Mark Wick.

On May 7, 2017, I got an email from a gentleman named Tom Allamanno in California. He was reaching out to me regarding the serial number on my frame. Months prior, I had joined the C&J Motorcycle Owners group on Facebook and posted pics of my serial number, asking if anyone knew what the numbers meant. If you recall, Jeff Cole of C&J had told me he didn't put those serial numbers on my frame, that his stamps had a different font. Tom stated that he had a Harley-Davidson XR750 frame with a serial number similar to mine and he was curious if I had ever found out what the numbers meant. He sent me some photos and sure enough, his serial number was D87824, while mine was D87840. This was the info I needed to push forward and find out the meaning of the number.

I took a screen shot of the XR750 serial number, #49's serial number, and the blurry picture of the water-cooled serial number and sent them out to the team members, hoping it would jog some memories. After a day, I got an email from John Ingham telling me to contact Steve Storz of Storz Performance. John had told me to reach out to Storz months before, when I had a question on the steering-stem lock nut. At that time, Steve could not help me, but I was hoping that this time he could.

I googled Steve Storz's name and I noticed on his company website a few photos of him working for Harley-Davidson as a mechanic. Then I found a cool video on Steve when he was inducted into the Trailblazer Motorcycle Club's Hall of Fame. I'd never heard of the Trailblazers before. On their website they say they are a social organization of pioneer motorcycle enthusiasts. Every year they induct influential people in the motorcycle industry into their Hall of Fame. They have been meeting annually since 1940. This sounded like a group I'd like to be a part of. The more I learned about Steve, the more I was in awe. I picked up the phone and gave him call.

Steve answered on the second ring. I reminded him of who I was and the project I was working on. I explained to him the serial number that was on my bike and how I had noticed a similar serial number on the water-cooled MX bike at the museum. I then told him about the third bike in California with the similar number. I added that I found it interesting that we had two bikes, one MX and one flat-track, with similar serial numbers. Steve couldn't answer as to why, so I told him I'd send him some pictures and let him think on it.

Within a day, I got an email back from Steve: "Keith, this is my recollection: D878 stands for Harley-Davidson's internal department number of the Racing Department (878). The additional digits correspond to a particular bike (or frame) that was used for racing or promotional purposes. It was probably necessary to have these numbers to track the sale or possession of these bikes, because they were not sold or transferred as production bikes. Sometimes they were given to riders when their contracts expired, other times not. Hope this helps, Steve."

There it was, the answer to the question that had been on my mind since I found the bike. The additional proof that the bike came from the race department was a welcome feeling. Tom Allamanno was equally happy when I relayed the information to him. He could now say he had a factory XR750 Harley-Davidson frame.

This was just the beginning of my experience with Steve Storz. His next email I found even more interesting: "As a side note, when I first started working for Harley-Davidson in July of 1976, I was temporarily assigned to work on the MX program alongside Don Habermehl and John Ingham. I also worked with Rex Staten (a really great guy BTW) at some of the Trans-AMA series in the fall of 1976. After that my good friend (and roommate) Tom Volin took over the MX duties. From 1977-78 I was a dirt track mechanic for Ted Boody, in 1979 Steve Morehead was my rider. Seems like only yesterday!"

So now I had connected another mechanic with the H-D MX team and had added another name to my team contact list. My next question for Steve was if he had any pictures from his time on the MX team.

He wasn't sure if he did or not, since he was with the MX team for such a short time. I searched through all my pics of the team and couldn't find any of Steve. That is, until I ran across a post by Steve Gustafson on Facebook. Just like that, within two months of Steve deciphering the serial number on #49, I located rare photos of him with Rex Staten at Unadilla, New York.

Rex and Steve behind the team truck at Unadilla, 1976. Photo by Steve Gustafson.

Rex and Steve at Unadilla, 1976. Photo by Steve Gustafson.

Steve working on Rex's bike. Notice the HOSS decal. Steve remembered welding
that bracket on the frame in this picture. Photo by Steve Gustafson.

I sent them to Steve right away so he could identify his bearded self: "Believe it or not, that's me with the beard! LOL. It was so cold in Milwaukee that I hated to shave in the morning, then have to go outside. So I grew a 'Milwaukee Face Warmer' during the winters."

I got permission from Steve Gustafson to post his pics and print some out to send to Steve Storz. In return, Steve Storz autographed a few of the pictures for me and also sent me some rare photos of Don Kudalski that were given out at the races. The photo of Kudalski I got from Steve was very interesting. I was able to track down the photographer and get permission to post it, but Harley-Davidson owns the rights. The photographer was Michael Havelin, and he started out in the mid-to-late 1970s taking pictures of MX riders around the East Coast. He said he had a stack of MX photos put away somewhere, but not to ask him to look for them because he probably couldn't find them. It was an awesome experience to connect with Steve and to learn so much about his history in motorcycle racing. I see now why he was inducted into the TrailBlazers' Hall of Fame.

DON KUDALSKI — #49 — HARLEY-DAVIDSON TEAM MOTOCROSS RIDER.   Photo by Mike Havelin

Photo of Don Kudalski that Steve Storz had kept from his days with Harley-Davidson. Used with permission of the Harley-Davidson Archives.

Steve was getting a kick out of my research and he sent me an email one day with a lead: "I have another research tip for you, although you may already know about this person. His name was Tim Dixon and he was not a Harley-Davidson employee, but was an outside contractor that was used as a kind of "gopher" for the MX team during those years. He would sometimes accompany Don or myself in the team truck for races and testing. He was really young, probably only 17 or 18 in 1976, but he was a real MX enthusiast. I have no idea how to contact him. Maybe Ingham or Habermehl could help. Not even sure what (if anything) he could help you with. Just thought I would mention him to you. SS."

My initial search for Tim Dixon didn't go well. There were hundreds of Tim Dixons out there and since I didn't even have a location to focus on, it was nearly impossible. It wasn't until months later, when I was in the process of tracking down Ricky O'Brien, that Dixon's name came up. Ricky's sister Terri knew the names of Tim's sisters. I tracked them down on Facebook and sent them messages. Within a day, one of them sent me Tim's email. Tim and I exchanged emails and set a date to talk. I emailed him a few pictures to get him thinking about his past. When Tim and I finally spoke, he was a wealth of knowledge.

Tim grew up in Lake Geneva, Wisconsin, where he and Eric Skrudland rode dirt bikes. Eric's father owned a local motorcycle shop. Don Habermehl said Eric's dad's shop supplied the first CR pipes the Harley-Davidson team modified and used on their race bikes. Eric raced motocross in high school and Tim was his mechanic.

Eric Skrudland's early #3 Harley-Davidson race bike in the 1975 season. Photo by James LaPaz.

Eric caught Harley-Davidson's eye when he took first in his district his senior year racing MX. Once they graduated from high school in 1975, Eric and Tim went to ride for Harley-Davidson. After riding and testing all summer, their first major race was in Florida at the Winter-AMA. Since Eric and Tim were both minors, their older friend Jeff Gracey had to take them. Eric injured his foot during the race and that was the end of his Harley-Davidson racing career, but Tim stayed with the team. It was a dream come true for the young Tim Dixon. He would travel the circuit with Don Habermehl, wrenching for Rex Staten and Ricky O'Brien in 1976 and then Rex Staten and Marty Tripes in 1977. Tim said that he would spend hours machining down cases to make them lighter. As he and Don traveled, they would pit at the major Harley-Davidson dealerships that were located near the races. It was common to have parts sent directly to the dealerships. Tim said that every week the bikes would be stripped, rebuilt, and repainted. This caught my attention right away, because it supported my finding of multiple paint layers on the #49 frame.

Tim told me of a time when he was in Florida and needed to sign his tax papers for the year, so the team flew him to Wisconsin where he met his parents at the airport, signed the papers and had lunch with them, then caught the next flight back to Miami. Tim said Rex Staten was a great guy to wrench for and an aggressive rider. He recalled that when Rex stayed at hotels, to stay in shape he would take a tall trash can and hop over it back and forth until he couldn't jump anymore. Another Rex story was about when they were in Rex's van on the way to a race and there was an eighteen-wheeler in front of them. Rex got on his CB and started making siren noises until the truck pulled over and Rex passed him and kept going.

Tim Dixon sitting on Rex Staten's bike at the gates. Photo by Lyndon Fox.

The last and final mechanic whom I stumbled across by accident took the whole team by surprise. I came across a picture from photographer Lyndon Fox. It was a photo of a 1977 team bike up against a pole with the seat and fender hanging loosely. In the background was a woman in a Harley-Davidson mechanic shirt, running towards the bike. At first, I figured she was someone's wife, but Tom Volin corrected me. The Harley-Davidson MX team employed a female mechanic for a brief period in 1977. She wrenched for Staten and Tripes and her name was Karen Germo. Since she was not a union mechanic, her stay was short, but that did not stop her from having a successful career in the road racing scene, working alongside famous engine builder Erv Kasemoto and wrenching for Gary Nixon.

I had to get in touch with her. With the help of Erv Kasemoto, I got her number. Karen was a pleasure to speak with. She talked about her days on the team and shared pictures of the Harley-Davidson race team jacket she still possessed. I searched and found a few more photos of Karen online and shared them with her.

Karen Germo in the background walking towards the camera. Photo by Lyndon Fox.

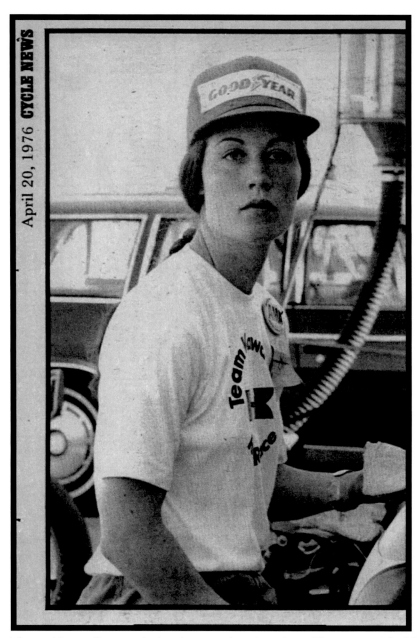

April 20, 1976 CYCLE NEWS

Cycle News article on Karen Germo during her road racing days. Photo provided by *Cycle News*.

CHAPTER 7

NOT GIVING UP

With the bike finished, there were still some unanswered questions. How did this bike make it to Missouri? And why were there production parts on it? The team members mentioned that they would visit or stay at the local dealerships near the tracks where they raced. With that in mind, I reached out to Ron Widman of Widman Harley-Davidson in St. Louis. Ron was now retired, but his brother still ran the shop. They were no longer an H-D dealership, but they still worked on bikes and their history with H-D was deeper than I had thought.

With Cycle World USA in St. Peters, Missouri, being the closest MX track near St. Louis, Ron told me that the MX team would stay at their shop when they were in town and that he once rode Rex Staten's motorcycle near the shop. I showed Ron pictures of my bike, but they did not ring a bell. "I don't know how they handled the MX team," he said. "The dirt trackers usually got to keep their bikes, but not always. The dirt trackers were quite normally assembled by the riders or tuner, a much looser association than the MX teams, which of course were sold by manufacturers as race replicas. I don't think the Harley-Davidson dealers ever had their heart in MX like the big four did."

I decided to visit their establishment to see if I could dig up any memories or artifacts. I got to meet Ron's brother Tom, who was now running the business. He didn't have much to share about my bike or the MX team. Both John Ingham and Clyde Denzer, though, remembered the Widmans.

When I told John Ingham that I visited Widman Harley-Davidson and that the MX team used their shop once, he said, "I don't remember using the shop, but Widman's son was the rider that ran the water-cooled prototype at Buchanan, Michigan. He and I also rode an enduro in Potosi, Missouri, before I started with the MX project."

This really surprised me because this was the first time I had heard John associate anything with Missouri and the water-cooled MX bike. I ran this information past Ron Widman, and he said it was not he who raced the water-cooled bike, but he did ride some enduros in Potosi. When Clyde Denzer was asked about the Widmans, he said, "I remember Earl Widman and his son Ron. Earl was instrumental in locating a manufacturer for the XR frames. The name of the manufacturer escapes me but they were located in St. Louis. The Harley-Davidson road race team would use Widman's shop on occasion when at the road race in Wentzville, Missouri."

I was close to getting answers with the Widmans, but it ended up being a dead end. I turned my attention back to Tricky Dick's and the Lillard family. I felt there was still something there. Jerry Lillard, owner of Tricky Dick's, had two sons: Andy and Sam. I decided to reach out to them through Facebook. Luckily, they answered my messages and they both were very welcoming. The older brother, Andy, could remember the bike being owned by the previous owner, but could not remember if it was sold through his father's business. They had records of every bike sold through the business, but in the early years his dad did not keep records.

They gave me the name of a brother-in-law of the previous owner, saying he might know something. After several attempts to contact him, I gave up. If #49 was sold through Tricky Dick's, it was early in the business when no records were kept.

Knowing that during Thanksgiving families get together, I reached out to John Ingham and his son Ken and told them to break out a photo album over the holidays and share some Harley-Davidson MX history. I was hoping that pictures of my bike might be discovered, but instead John showed Ken some cool pictures of pre-prototype MX designs and blueprints to the Cagiva bikes of 1979. John worked briefly for Cagiva when they were transitioning from Aermacchi. These photos brought up a great discussion on the Facebook group, like the story Ken told about John's rear fork design. The rear fork/shocks the team used on the 1975 model were designed by the team engineer, John. Rumor has it that his suspension design was what eventually led to the Fox air shock. The group members also learned that the original race frames for the 1975 MX bikes were made in-house and welded by race department welder Ralph Berndt. The team would eventually switch to a Champion MX frame and finally to frames from C&J. There were some awesome pictures that Ken shared with the Harley-Davidson MX Owners group on Facebook, but there were still no additional clues to #49.

One good thing about joining groups on Facebook is that you never know what's going to pop up, and that's exactly what happened on the Harley-Davidson MX Owners page. One day, a new member, Dan Goldman, posted pictures of a massive score of MX parts he found. Apparently, the guy he got them from had factory connections. What he had was a factory team radial head—not just any head, but the head I needed for the #49 bike. What was odd was that he had this head on a 1975 MX250 lower end, so the two didn't go together. The good news was that I had the head that matched his lower end and he had the head that matched what Kudalski raced. I reached out to Dan immediately to see what his plans were and explained to him the different year parts on his motor. Since it was hard to put a price on my 1975 MX head and his radial head, we agreed on an even trade. This was a big deal for both of us and a big hurdle in making my #49 bike 100 percent complete. Even though I had just fabricated a matching head for #49, having the real head was the cherry on top. Now, those purchases from the bike shop in Arkansas came into play....

Newly acquired 1978 radial team head. Photo by Keith Geisner.

With the factory Harley-Davidson radial head in my possession, I was on top of the world. These heads were extremely rare. So was the head I traded, but I didn't have a bike that matched the 1975 MX head. I still had four prototype cylinders I had purchased in Arkansas, and I knew Dan also needed a prototype cylinder to go along with the head and lower end of his motor.

I had these cylinders stored in my shop attic. I got them down and took a look at them to see which one I would set aside for Dan. I had three that were unused old stock and one that was used. Out of the three NOS cylinders, one looked totally different, which kind of caught me off guard. It looked as though someone had done a great job trimming down the fins, and a boost port had been added above the intake. I decided to take pictures of it next to another one for comparison and then I sent them to the team for examination. The response I received opened the door to the remainder of my research.

I got an email from Don Habermehl in response to my cylinder question. Don's email simply said: "Call me the next time you're next to those cylinders." It had been over a year since I had spoken to Don on the phone and I felt like I had been bugging the crap out of him with my emails. To have him ask me to call him was out of the ordinary. When I phoned him, Don had two questions: "Are the head stud holes in the cylinder ¼"-20 Heli coils?" and "Is there a boost port above the intake?" When I answered in the affirmative to both questions, Don replied that the cylinder was one that he had modified. This floored me, but I made sense out of it.

These cylinders were from 39 Cycles near Eureka Springs, Arkansas. Back in the late '70's, Rich, the owner of 39 Cycles, moved from Milwaukee, Wisconsin, to Arkansas, taking three tractor-trailer loads of Harley-Davidson Aermacchi parts and bikes with him. At one time, Rich must have gotten a load of factory Harley-Davidson race department parts and kept them the whole time until I came around. This was all great news, and it was a most enjoyable talk I had with Don. What were the chances that after forty years I would run across the #49 bike and these parts from Arkansas that were originally from the Harley-Davidson race department? Up to this point, I had been adding race team members to the Harley-Davidson MX250 Facebook Owners group so they could see my updates on the bike and post answers to group members' questions. After this phone call with Don, I added him to the group and he really opened up.

Around this same time, I reached out to a gentleman on eBay who was selling Harley-Davidson MX parts. I noticed he was from around Springfield, Illinois. He told me that he had quite a few parts and that he had been into flat-track racing MX250s back in the day. I found out he had three prototype heads that had come out of the Harley-Davidson race department. I had him send me some photos of the heads and I shared them with Don. The heads had scribing on the sides, which I found intriguing. "I did the scribing," Don replied. "Guess I have to admit. For a while, I would note the thickness of the head gasket the motor used and the amount of cc the head was then off to the dyno we'd go. Good luck, Don."

Now, knowing these were actual heads Don modified, I made a deal with the guy and purchased all three. When the heads showed up, one perfectly matched the trimmed-down cylinder I had that Don had modified. What were the chances that after forty years this head and cylinder would come together once again? Don also told me that he had modified approximately four cylinders with reed cages for use by the MX team.

Don Habermehl-modified cylinder and matching head come together after forty years. Photo by Keith Geisner.

Non-trimmed cylinder with a Don Habermehl-modified head. Photo by Keith Geisner.

By adding Don Habermehl to the Harley-Davidson MX250 Owners group on Facebook, I now had almost the whole team on there. John Ingham, Steve Storz, Tom Volin's wife, Don Kudalski's wife, Eric Skrudland, Rex Staten, Scott Wallenberg, and now Don Habermehl. Around this same time, John Ingam's son Ken posted pictures of what he and John had looked at over Thanksgiving and Don added some informative comments to the post. It really got the other team members talking and people were asking questions. One important question was posted that got me thinking again about how the #49 bike made it to Missouri. A group member asked John Ingham if Don Kudalski ever raced the water-cooled bike. I answered "no" without thinking, based on my conversations with Kudalski. Don never raced the water-cooled bike. Ingham brought up that the water-cooled bike was raced at Red Bud MX in Buchanan, Michigan, by a guy from Missouri. This got me thinking and I even replied to Ingham, saying, "I wonder if that's how the #49 bike made it to Missouri?"

I followed up my response with a quick message to Kudalski, asking if he ever raced the water-cooled bike. He replied: "Good afternoon Keith; one week before the national at Red Bud MX, Harley ask me to test the water-cooled bike and maybe race it. The bike had a flat spot in the power band that no one could fix, so I ran the air-cooled bike and was winning the first moto until the bike broke. It was a muddy race track and son of a gun if the water-cooled bike finished that day. They found someone to ride it, but I don't remember who he was, sorry." I followed up with a phone call to Tom Volin, who also confirmed it was a guy from around St. Louis who raced the water-cooled bike in 1978.

All this talk about a local pro from St. Louis who could have ridden the Harley-Davidson water-cooled MX bike got me thinking about the people I personally knew around St. Louis who were racing pro back then. Off the top of my head, I knew of two guys, Craig Mueller and Jay Clark. I first reached out to Craig Mueller, because he had a lot of information about the St. Peters track, which was called Cycle World USA back in the day. Craig could not think of anyone. Next I tried Jay Clark. I actually worked with Jay Clark, so it was pretty easy to get in touch with him. I told Jay my story and, based on the location of the bike when I found it, he came up with one name. The name ended up not being the needle in the haystack, but it was nice to reach out to the guy and talk about old bikes and the current preservation I was doing.

Craig Mueller battling Rich Eierstedt and Rex Staten at Cycle World USA in St. Peters, Missouri, 1977. Photo by Craig Mueller.

Jay Clark airing it out in 1974. Photo by Jay Clark.

The next day was a little more exciting. I called Jay and told him more about where and when the water-cooled bike was raced. I told him it was raced in July 1978 at Red Bud in Buchanan, Michigan, and that I had made several internet searches to find the results of the Red Bud race. Everywhere I looked, they only listed the top twenty riders. Jay replied, "Hey, I raced in that race!" He had made the top twenty and had beaten Marty Tripes. The best part was that Jay believed he still had the program from the race—which would have listed all the riders who had pre-entered. He said he would look for it that night and get back with me. Needless to say, I could barely sleep knowing that I might get the answer to my biggest question about the bike.

Before I tell you about what Jay found, I want to briefly share another story. If you have never visited the Mungenast Classic Automobiles & Motorcycles Museum in St. Louis, I highly recommend it. It is the coolest motorcycle museum in town. I was at their Supercross party back in March 2017, when I first met and spoke with Ray Mungenast about #49. Unfortunately, Ray knew nothing of the bike, but he was familiar with the Harley-Davidson MX team and found my story to be interesting.

Meeting Ray for the first time was an awesome experience. He and his family had a deep history in motorcycle racing. I told Ray that I would keep him posted on my progress. Fast forward to December 2017, when the Mungenast Museum was having its annual Christmas party. I was excited to talk with Ray again and update him on the completion of the bike and also tell him about finding Jim Simmons' 1976 ISDT Husqvarna I had acquired back in October. To my surprise, Ray not only rode occasionally with Simmons, but he also was a friend of his daughter April. Ray's dad, Dave Sr., also raced in the ISDT with Jim.

"Keith," Ray said, "you didn't find these bikes—these bikes found you." I had never thought of it that way, but I loved old motorcycles and I was determined to see that the histories of the two bikes were preserved. I took the opportunity to ask Ray if I could display the #49 bike at his family's museum during the 2018 Supercross party, and he said I could, most definitely. Ray didn't know it, but it had been a dream of mine to display a bike at their museum. It is seemingly fate how the rest of the story unfolded....

Back to Jay Clark. The next morning after we spoke, I got an instant message from Jay, saying he had some information for me. I quickly messaged him back to get the news. Jay said there were two other people on the Red Bud MX race program who had raced for Harley-Davidson. One was Tracy Nichols of Columbia, Missouri, sponsored by Nichols Harley-Davidson, and the other was Gary Stroud of Indiana. I found it curious that there were two other riders racing for Harley-Davidson in that race.

The first thing I did was a quick Google check on the names. Nothing easy came up on Tracy Nichols, but Gary Stroud popped up instantly. He appeared to be the owner of Gary Stroud Racing in Porter County, Indiana. Gary was very gracious on the phone and happy to talk about his past racing experiences. I mentioned that he was listed in the Red Bud MX race program, and he replied that he did have a production MX250 that he had raced that year, but at Red Bud MX he had switched to a Maico last-minute. The people at Red Bud MX didn't update the program. I told him about my discovery of #49, but he had no information to offer me. He had sold his production MX bike years ago, but he did have an NOS pair of Harley-Davidson MX pants. I asked if he was willing to sell them and we agreed on a price. After I thanked Gary for his time, I messaged Jay and gave him the update. Tracy Nichols had to be my guy. I needed more research to find him.

Jay Clark's race program. Image used with permission from AMA Pro.

CHAPTER 8

THE NICHOLS BROTHERS

I started digging deeper online for Tracy Nichols. I found one website that was a dedication page to Tracy that one of his friends had put together. I could see he had a history of racing MX and then later circle track racing cars. The person who put this website together had a contact email, so I sent him a message requesting Tracy's contact information. Meanwhile, I was still digging on Facebook and I ran across a page that had Tracy's contact information on it. If this was the guy who raced the water-cooled bike for the team at Red Bud MX, he might know how #49 made it back to Missouri. Would the team have given him the bike to practice with? I would soon find out....

For the rest of the day, I thought of questions to ask Tracy. In the back of my mind, I was thinking I had to be careful not to say too much at first, in case the bike was stolen. I had to plan my questions carefully to get as much information out of him without making him suspicious. This turned out to be the longest day ever. Needless to say, I wasn't very productive at work: to think that there was a chance that I could get all my questions answered after fourteen months of calls, emails and instant messages. There was also a chance I could be discovering Harley-Davidson history that had gone unnoticed by the public, due to the MX team disbanding at the end of the 1978 season.

When I got home that evening, I explained to my wife about the important phone call I had to make and she agreed to keep the kids in the basement during this time. I sat down at the kitchen table and dialed Tracy's number. It was January 25, 2018.

The phone rang a few times before Tracy answered. I said "Hello" and introduced myself. I told Tracy I was doing research on the Harley-Davidson motocross team and his name came up in my research when I saw that he had ridden a Harley-Davidson in the Red Bud MX National in July 1978. Right away, Tracy replied, "Yes, that was me. I actually got to race the Harley-Davidson team's water-cooled bike in that race."

When I heard his words, *my* heart started to race! I asked how he was able to pull that off and he proceeded to tell me his story. Tracy's parents had owned Nichols Harley-Davidson in Columbia, Missouri. Tracy had been racing MX for several years leading up to the 1978 season. His older brother Terry was his mechanic. In 1978, the Harley-Davidson MX production bike hit dealers' showrooms and Tracy started racing the production bikes. He said they would always reach out to the Harley-Davidson race team for parts and tips to make his production bike better. If the team was ever racing at Cycle World USA in St. Peters, sometimes they would send the Nichols parts for them to deliver to the track. All that communication and assistance with the team paid off at Buchanan, Michigan, in the July 1978 Red Bud MX National race. Tracy and his brother Terry went to race their production bike. When they got to the race, team project engineer

John Ingham asked them if they would be interested in debuting the Harley-Davidson MX water-cooled bike. At this point, the team members were familiar with the Nichols brothers, and since Don "Killer" Kudalski decided to race his air-cooled bike instead, it would be a shame not to see this bike in action. This was not an invitation you would refuse, so Tracy leapt at the opportunity.

The debut of the Harley-Davidson water-cooled MX bike at Red Bud MX Buchanan, Michigan - 250 National, 1978. Raced by Tracy Nichols. Photo by Jim Gianatsis/FastDates.com.

The Red Bud MX National was a very muddy race. Tracy said that he got so much mud in his eyes he ended up scratching his cornea. He finished the race, but not in the top twenty, while Kudalski's bike broke down. I asked if that was the only time he had raced the water-cooled bike, and he said "Yes." I pointed out that he was probably the only person ever to race that bike in competition and told him that the bike was currently in the Harley-Davidson Museum in Milwaukee. Tracy replied that he and his brother had been curious as to whatever had happened to that bike. He said they had only recently talked about it. His next words took me by surprise.

Tracy said that he had had a Kudalski team bike at one time. I didn't say anything at first, because Tracy went on to tell me that the family's dealership ended up closing and everything went into storage. I questioned him about the Kudalski MX team bike and where it was today. He repeated that the Kudalski bike went into storage when his parents' dealership closed and he couldn't remember much more about it— other than that he wished he still had it. Tracy went on to say that at the end of the 1978 season, when the Harley-Davidson MX team ended, Clyde Denzer reached out to them to see if they would be interested in any MX parts from the race department. That's when they acquired the Kudalski bike. Tracy added that his brother, Terry, would remember more about the bike, since he himself had sustained several head injuries during his racing career. I asked Tracy if he had any pictures of the bike, and he texted me one. There it was, the same bike I had, only in newer condition.

As I looked down at the photo Tracy sent me, I studied it closely, just as I had done a thousand times over the past year when I came across any new photo of a Harley-Davidson MX team bike. This *was* my bike! It had the stock shocks, the solid aluminum rear sprocket, and the same font numbers and plastic. I was curious about the stock shocks—would the Nichols brothers have received the bike from the team with stock shocks? I asked Tracy if I could give his brother a call and ask him a few questions. He didn't hesitate giving me his number. I told Tracy I'd phone him back after speaking with Terry.

I called Terry and introduced myself the same way I did with Tracy. I reiterated what his brother had told me so far, telling him that I needed some clarification on a few things. Terry confirmed that the Red Bud MX race was the only time they raced the water-cooled bike for the team. Their next encounter with the team took place at the end of the season. He said they were invited up to the race department to grab what they wanted. They took their van and grabbed anything they could, including a nearly complete Kudalski bike. Terry told me that he almost got an MX360 motor, but that at the last minute someone in the race department took it back. Terry went on to say that he snagged a Turner pipe and a custom reed cylinder as well.

On the way home, Tracy drove while Terry was in the back of the van putting the bike together. By the time they got home, if any parts were missing they would pull them off Tracy's production race bike. That answered my question as to how #49 got a production motor, shocks, and tank strap. This was great information in solving the mystery behind #49, but I still needed to know how it ended up in that barn in Shelbina, Missouri.

I asked Terry whatever happened to Kudalski's bike, and he reiterated what Tracy had told me—that after his family closed the dealership, they had put everything in storage. The owner of the storage units also owned a grocery store in Columbia by the name of Randy's Market. To help pay for storage, Terry and Tracy's father gave the Kudalski bike to the storage unit owner. Terry said he believed the next owner rode it in a hare scramble, but then the bike ended up in a shop that specialized in three-wheelers. I asked Terry if that shop was named Tricky Dick's and if it had been in Shelbina, and he believed that information was correct, but not 100 percent. Regardless of how #49 made it to me, the path on how #49 made it to Missouri was now solved. I was on pins and needles.

I asked Terry if the bike had ever been stolen, and he replied that it had not and that it was probably long-gone in a scrapyard somewhere. I asked him again if there was any possibility the bike was stolen, and he again said no, neither from him nor from the owners after him.

"Terry," I said, "I have the Kudalski bike."

There was dead silence on the other end of the phone. Terry again said that there was no way and the bike was no longer around.

"No, Terry," I replied, "I have the bike. It's been in a barn in Shelbina, Missouri, since the mid-1980s and I purchased it back in September of 2016. I've spent the last year and a half researching the bike and preserving it." I told him that after talking with him and his brother, my research as to the bike's history had officially ended. As I had him on the phone, I texted him photos of the bike on the bike stand with the jerseys behind it. Terry was stunned. I further told him about connecting with all the former team members and my efforts to restore the bike to its original racing condition, noting that all the stock parts that they had used from Tracy's production bike were replaced with factory team parts, except for the motor, which was still the same one off Tracy's bike. All of a sudden, Terry's phone started blowing up with calls from Tracy. I told Terry I had better call Tracy back to explain. Terry thanked me as I hung up.

I called Tracy back and he sounded humbled. He asked where I had found that bike and I told him I had held off until I could make sure the bike hadn't been stolen. I told him my history with the bike. Tracy said that he recognized the tank strap because it was one of the parts the team had sent to them to have delivered to the Cycle World USA race in St. Peters. He was amazed that the bike was still in existence and now preserved. I told him I would share photos and I thanked him for his time. He expressed his gratitude for my reaching out to them. Harley-Davidson MX history was now uncovered, and now it was time to let the world know.

Terry Nichols standing next to #49 after returning from the Harley-Davidson race department. Photo by Tracy and Terry Nichols.

As soon as I got off the phone with Tracy, I started writing the story down to share with the Harley-Davidson MX250 Owners group on Facebook. I had been waiting a year and a half to tell this story, and I couldn't believe how it had all gone down. No sooner than I posted the story to the group than John Ingham replied and corrected my statement that it had been Clyde Denzer who had offered the water-cooled bike to Tracy. Rather, John had been the one. I corrected that error quickly. John summed up my story by commenting: "That is about as accurate as you can be on an event that was forty years ago." Clyde Denzer commented, "Keith, I do not believe anyone can enjoy this story as much as you. There are several folks doing research on various Harley-Davidson subjects. They, as you, are very dedicated and exacting in the data they collect. It has always impressed me that you folks are so determined to get facts correct. During the days of our working in the racing department, we never gave a thought to our making history. Thanks to you and others like you, some of it will be recorded and preserved. Thank you, and congratulations on a task well done. Clyde."

Not only did I connect the dots on the #49 bike, but I unveiled a piece of Harley-Davidson MX history that was forgotten. Tracy Nichols was the only person to race the water-cooled Harley-Davidson MX bike in AMA competition. What a story! It was crazy how everything came together during the preservation— but the surprises weren't over yet.

CHAPTER 9

TREASURES IN THE ATTIC

Around this same time, I got an interesting email from Don Habermehl. Don explained that they had recently sold their old house to one of his sons. His son went to insulate the attic above the garage and discovered a bunch of Harley-Davidson MX team parts stashed away. Don included photos of what his son had found, which included a couple of Cross Up swingarms, a complete lower end, a pipe, a gear set, bars, and some miscellaneous stuff. I noticed the lower end had the team serial number stamped on it. I knew right away that I had to have that lower end to make the #49 bike complete, so I gave Don a call. I explained to Don that I needed that lower end and why. The stamp font Harley-Davidson used for their serial numbers was under lock and key, so to find a lower end stamped with the serial number the race team would have used was super rare, and in my case the chance of a lifetime to match it with the #49 bike. Race team engine serial numbers started with 7D180xxH7 for the 250cc and 1G400xxH6 for the 341cc; 7D18 and 1G40 meant "race department" and the digit after the "H" was the year. In comparison, production MX motor VIN numbers were stamped 7D10xxxH7 and over-the-counter replacement cases were stamped 7D90xxxH7. The 7D10 was a production motor stamp and 7D90 meant over-the-counter replacements.

I had also noticed the swingarms Don had. The design of the chain adjuster mounts on one of the swingarms was just like mine, but the other swingarm chain adjuster mounts were "beefier looking"—like most of what the team had used. Don's reply was that the one that looked like mine was the original design that they got from Cross Up. They were afraid the chain adjuster mount design wasn't strong enough, so they made their own swingarm in the race department and had Cross Up copy it—and that was the design most of the team used. That swingarm was the other swingarm Don had. It was steel and made in the race department.

Comparison of the chain adjuster mounts. This original Cross Up swingarm was painted orange, the race department-made swingarm is bare metal. Photo by Keith Geisner.

I was blown away by this information. It was the final question that needed answering on my bike. Throughout the preservation process, I had planned on making a trip to Milwaukee with #49. Since Don didn't want to ship all those parts, it made sense to schedule my trip, meet Don in person, show him the bike—and stop in at the Harley-Davidson museum.

Don and I discussed our meet-up and how we might make a weekend of it. We wanted to hit the museum and see the water-cooled bike, and maybe show off #49 as well. After a couple of emails to my previous museum contact, I learned that all 2018 events were booked up. I hated to take the bike all the way up there and not be able to show it or tell its story.

After a week of trying to get assistance from the museum, Don called me and told me about his good friend, Peter Zlystra, who had been a draftsman for the race team. He had told Peter my story and Peter told him I should write a letter to the museum's director, Bill Davidson.

At first, I was a bit intimidated. Bill Davidson was motorcycle royalty, after all, being the great-grandson of the co-founder of Harley-Davidson. It appeared to be my only hope, though, so I began drafting my letter to the son of Willie G Davidson. My wife, Sara, assisted me:

January 21, 2018

Dear Mr. Davidson:

My name is Keith Geisner and I live near St. Louis, MO. Back in September 2016, I purchased what I thought was a 1978 Harley-Davidson MX250, but this was no typical production MX250. I quickly learned it was a factory Harley-Davidson race team bike. More specifically, a #49 Don

Kudalski back-up bike. Over the next year, I performed a preservation restoration on the bike, at the same time contacting every member of the race team— including "Killer" Kudalski—to gain details on the bike and team.

That brings us to today, where we are only a few weeks away from the 40th anniversary of Harley-Davidson's only motocross win—by #49 Don Kudalski—and the last year Harley-Davidson raced motocross.

In the next few weeks, I will be scheduling a visit with MX team lead mechanic Don Habermehl in Milwaukee. I want to finally meet Don in person and bring him and the #49 bike back together again.

The reason I'm writing you is to see if the museum would be interested in this visit to commemorate the 40th anniversary of Harley-Davidson's last season in motocross and the only win in Harley-Davidson's motocross history. I thought you might be interested in an article for one of your publications or sites – or to host us for a special tour of your museum. I'm not asking for anything more – just a chance to bring the bike full circle.

Enclosed please find a few pictures of the team bike I preserved this year. Looking forward to my visit to Milwaukee and the Harley-Davidson museum. I would love an opportunity to share this piece of Harley-Davidson's motocross history with you.

Please feel free to call or email me at your convenience. I really appreciate your time and consideration.

Sincerely,
Keith Geisner

Within a week of mailing the letter, I received a voicemail from Bill Davidson. His message sent chills down my spine. Not only did he invite me to bring #49 to the Harley-Davidson museum, but I learned that Bill had a MX bike as well that he had received from the team. I waited a few days before returning Bill's call. That same week, Harley-Davidson had released earnings and announced it would be closing its Kansas City, Missouri, plant. When I finally called and left a message, his assistant Dara Greene got in touch with me by email setting the date and time to be at the museum.

Wow! This was really going to happen. I began considering how many people I would take along on this historic occasion. There would be at least three: Don, Sara and myself. The more I thought about it, I needed to reach out to the team members to see if any of them would want to attend. In another case of serendipity, the visit was scheduled in the week of the 40th anniversary of Don "Killer" Kudalski's only Harley-Davidson motocross team win. I sent out a group email.

Teammates,

I've reached out to Bill Davidson and he responded with much excitement to visit with me and the #49 bike the morning of 2/23/18 at the museum. Don Habermehl and Clyde Denzer will also be attending. I wouldn't feel right not reaching out to the rest of you to see if you'd like to meet as well. You'd have to provide your own travel, but when at the museum we will meet with Bill Davidson for an hour or so, and then get to go on a tour. I'm hoping Bill brings in his team bike and also breaks out the water-cooled bike for a photo opportunity. This all came together this week so let me know your decision as soon as possible. Just a coincidence that week is the 40th

anniversary of Kudalski's only Harley-Davidson MX win! I hope we can all meet up. I'm driving up Thursday 2/22 and the meeting is at 10:30 am Friday morning 2/23.

Let me know,
Keith

By the end of the week, I received RSVPs from everyone on the team. Tom Volin and Clyde Denzer were the only ones going, but the rest of the team sent their thanks and well-wishes.

The weeks leading up to the 23rd flew by. The week before the trip, I had watched my nephew Nathan wrestle in the Missouri State High School tournament in Columbia. He battled his way to third place and we were all super proud. While I was there, I texted the Nichols brothers, who lived in Columbia, and let them know about the museum visit. I told them I would share their stories with Bill Davidson, and they in turn wished me the best. The year 2018 was off to a roaring start.

Leading up to February 23, I stayed in contact with Bill Davidson's assistant, Dara. I was persistent in reminding her how cool it would be to get the water-cooled bike, Bill's team bike, and my #49 bike together for a photo. When I heard back from her, she said that everything was on schedule, but that they couldn't move the water-cooled bike out of the archives and that Bill's bike was too far off-site.

My next question for Dara was how I was going to display #49 when I got there? I envisioned having the bike on display when Bill arrived. I would then leave it on display until the tour was over. She replied that she would have to get back to me.

By the week of the trip I had everything on my end in order, including an insurance policy on the bike and a rented U-Haul trailer. I also packed a few items for the team members to sign, including a 1976 H-D MX team gas tank, a 1975 MX/SX mag cover and a photo album I had put together of the bike in various stages of preservation. I wanted to take a gift to Bill Davidson as well, and I had the perfect gift for the guy who likely had everything Harley-Davidson: a replica MX team stand for his bike. I doubted he had one of those.

Thursday morning came and I had everything loaded into the U-Haul, including my barriers in case the bike would be displayed, along with my tools and a can of Fix-a-Flat. I was anxious about any troubles along the way. Tom Volin was flying in from Oregon and meeting us in Milwaukee. I still hadn't heard back from Dara by the time Sara and I hit the road.

Along the way, dinner reservations were made with Don and his wife, Mary Ann, Tom, Sara and me. We arrived at our hotel around four in the afternoon. While Sara and I were getting settled in, I received a message from Dara stating that there would be a place to display the bike outside the entrance of the museum, a gated area where they usually displayed next year's models. This was great news!

I met up with Tom Volin at our hotel. His room was on the same floor, so we met up and rode the elevator down to the lobby together. Meeting Tom was a huge event for me. I asked him if I could record our conversation. Here was a man who had ridden for Husqvarna in the '60s and '70s—he had been around people like Malcolm Smith and Steve McQueen. After his stint with H-D, he had gone on to work for Yamaha. I had so many questions I wanted to ask.

In the hotel lobby, I let Tom look through my picture book. I let him go through it at his own pace. Tom confirmed the Turner pipe on one of Rex Staten's #31 bikes I had a picture of and also the pipe on #49. He was friends with the Turner brothers from California, and it was he who had ordered the Turner-made pipes for the team. Tom also told me about when he had first come to Harley-Davidson to work, in the winter of 1976. He drove his Chevy El-Camino from Oregon to Wisconsin in one of the worst winters ever. He said the morning after he arrived in Milwaukee, his car wouldn't move due to the rear axle oil being coagulated. He had to use a plumber's torch to heat it up.

Tom also brought along his camera and showed me photos of some of his projects. I was pleased to learn that his father owned a body shop like my dad. Tom still wrenched on cars. He showed me pics of his old Chevy ton truck that he was making into a fuel delivery truck. He also had pics of an old Triumph desert racer his uncle used to race. I told him my uncle had raced as well.

Tom gave me his Harley-Davidson Team mechanic card that he had had to keep with him at AMA events. I told him I would cherish it always. Before we left to meet up with Don, I had Tom sign my photo album.

The group met up at Meyer's Restaurant. It was great to finally meet Don and Mary Ann. Don promptly began to interview me about my own motorcycle history. I eventually produced the photo album so he could look it over. Once again, I asked permission to record our conversations.

As we discussed the various stages of #49's preservation, I asked about the story behind the finned mag covers on the 1976-77 Harley-Davidson MX team bikes. According to Don, finned mag covers weren't for decoration. They were having problems with the Dansi ignition rotor breaking the left-side crank at high RPM. To fix this issue, Don made a crank out of two right-hand crank halves because the right-hand half had a thicker shaft. He modified the Dansi rotor to mount backwards onto the crank. He then took the stator off the left-hand motor case and mounted it on the inside of the mag cover. For him to be able to do this, the mag cover had to be extremely modified to position the stator just right with the rotor. The genius design fixed their ignition problem until the introduction of the Moto Plat ignition system in 1977.

Habermehl-modified crank that fixed the Dansi ignition woes and mag cover modified per Habermehl's directions. Photo by Keith Geisner.

Tom shared an interesting story about Don. The team would use Harley-Davidson orange spray bomb in the race department to paint parts for the team bikes. Due to the cold weather, mechanics would place the spray cans on a hot plate to allow the paint to warm up. There was one instance when Don left his spray can on the hot plate for too long, causing it to blow up. Luckily no one was injured, but the event gave Don the nickname "Don the Bomb." I heard a few more stories by other race department members of fires and explosions Don had caused while working on his lathe that I won't get into, but the nickname was fitting.

On the way to the museum the next morning, I was a nervous wreck. The roads in Milwaukee are rough and it felt like I was hitting every pothole that came our way. However, we made it to the museum with no problems. I pulled up right in front where Dara had told me to unload. The display area was perfect. As Tom and I met at the back of the trailer, Dara came out to meet us. It was great to finally meet her in person. We introduced ourselves and Dara pointed to the display area where I could show the bike. It was just before 10 a.m., and Bill Davidson was scheduled to arrive at 10:30. Dara said she'd meet us inside once we were set up, so Tom and I started unloading the trailer. I first pulled out a storage box that had the 1976 MX team gas tank I brought for autographs, along with my picture book and magneto cover. Then I pulled out the bike stand and put it in place inside the display area. Lastly, I pulled the #49 bike out and placed it onto the stand. Oh, what a glorious moment! All of my hard work had paid off and my bike was standing proudly on display in front of the Harley-Davidson Museum!

#49 on display front in of the Harley-Davidson Museum. Photo by Keith Geisner.

Sara and I pulled the truck behind the museum. As we walked away from the truck, we saw a man on the sidewalk waiting for us. He introduced himself as Clyde Denzer. I was beyond excited to meet the former manager of the Harley-Davidson MX team.

Clyde walked with us to the museum entrance. The museum was opening and visitors were arriving, stopping to view #49 and ask questions. We walked inside the lobby and before long Don Habermehl showed up, along with Brent Thompson and Peter Zlystra. Brent had also been a mechanic inside the race department and Peter, as mentioned earlier, was a draftsman as well as the designer of the XR750.

As I looked around the lobby of the museum, I was in awe. It was great to see the team members all talking and catching up on old times. At that moment, I pulled out the gas tank, mag cover, and photo book and had all the guys sign them. As the guys were signing my items, Dara told us to look up. An electronic message board read "Welcome Keith and Sara."

We still had twenty minutes before Bill's arrival, so we took a trip upstairs to view the bikes. Peter took Sara around and explained the various exhibits while Clyde showed me some photos I had sent him of the front brake cable guide on the front fender. He said I had hit the nail on the head: the brake guide looked exactly like the one the team had used. I was overjoyed that Clyde took the time to mention this to me.

By the time we made it back down to the lobby, there was a group of people out front looking at the #49 bike. One man approached me and wanted to know all about it. I gave him the name of the Facebook group to join so he could read about the history of the bike. As I stood there, taking it all in, another employee of Harley-Davidson joined us. It was Tim McCormick, the museum's communications project manager. He and my wife, Sara, had something in common: they had both graduated from the University of Missouri School of Journalism.

When Bill Davidson appeared, I was shaking as I shook his hand. I told him about my journey with #49 and let him know about Tracy Nichols being the only rider ever to ride in competition the water-cooled bike now in his museum. We talked for some time until I remembered his gift. I excused myself and ran to get it.

As I made my way back into the lobby, I was able to sneak the stand back behind Dara and Tim as Bill was catching up with the team members. When Bill turned and saw the stand, his face lit up. He said the photos I had sent of my bike stand had reminded him of his original stand that he still had, but that it was so far gone there was no way he would put his bike on it. I assured him his bike would be safe on my stand. After giving the bike stand to a museum official, Bill looked over my memorabilia and signed all of it. Finally, we went outside to view the bike.

Bill Davidson and I checking out #49. Photo by Keith Geisner.

At first it was just Bill and I walking up to the bike as everyone else hung back. Bill told me he wished he had brought his bike in. Soon, the rest of the team joined us. We all lined up and took a group photo with the bike. For me, this was the "money shot." I would treasure it always. Bill and I shook hands once more and got a photo with us standing by the bike, with the team members in the background.

L to R: Tom Volin, Keith Geisner, Don Habermehl, Peter Zlystra, Brent Thompson, Bill Davidson and Clyde Denzer. Photo by Keith Geisner.

Don and Tom inspecting my work. Photo by Keith Geisner.

It was time for the museum tour. We began with the very first Harley-Davidson motorcycle (Harley-Davidson #1) and made our way to archives while listening to Bill and discussing various topics concerning the history of the company. When we arrived at archives, everyone scattered and looked at all the various vintage bikes. The water-cooled MX bike was on the top row of some storage racks, out of reach, but it could be easily viewed. I was hoping for a close-up look, but when I looked around me at all the people who had come together over #49, it really didn't matter.

We spent two hours touring the museum and then it was time to bid some people farewell. Brent, Clyde and Peter said their goodbyes and then Tom, Don, Sara and I headed over to the museum restaurant.

We put our names in for the 45-minute wait. All at once Bill appeared and asked what we were doing. When I told him we were waiting to be seated, he motioned to us to follow him. I went and retrieved Sara and Tom from the gift shop and we followed Bill into the restaurant. Talk about feeling like VIPs! We were going to have lunch with Bill Davidson!

After being around Bill for two hours, my anxiety was starting to wear off. Over an excellent meal, we discussed business, hobbies, and life in general. When Bill picked up the tab, I was touched.

After lunch, Sara and I said goodbye to Bill. It was time to load up #49 and Tom and Don jumped in to help. When I pulled around with the truck, I saw Tom pushing the bike over and I immediately stopped to take a picture; it had been forty years since Tom had pushed a team bike around. Once we were loaded, Tom headed back to our hotel and Don went home. Sara and I took one final lap through the museum.

Tom Volin loading up #49 like he did forty years earlier. Photo by Keith Geisner.

I took Sara back to our hotel and then headed to Don's house to pick up the parts I was getting from him. The parts were everything I needed to put #49 back in 100 percent team condition. Don ended up giving me the parts, and I was overwhelmed with his generosity. The parts included a team motor lower end, a 1976 Honda CR250 pipe that the team used on the '76 team bikes, K&N handlebars, MX360 transmission, an original Cross Up swingarm (exactly what was on the #49 bike), and a race department-made Cross Up copy swingarm made out of steel in case the aluminum swingarms weren't strong enough, which I had learned about earlier.

One of the wooden boxes the Harley-Davidson MX team used to transport their motors. Team motor inside. Photo by Keith Geisner.

Extra parts donated to #49. Photo by Keith Geisner.

The next morning Sara and I had breakfast with Tom before hitting the road for home. I told him I had received an email from Clyde Denzer:

> *Keith and Sara, thank you so much. It was a great day! Meeting the both of you was such a pleasure. Keith, you have done a spectacular job on the bike. It is very, very impressive. It was obvious that we were all impressed. I also thank you for arranging the meeting. I have not seen or talked to Tom since he left Harley-Davidson. The bonds that develop within a race team never leave us and it was so enjoyable to renew with Tom. The members of the Harley-Davidson race team changed with the programs but every member became part of the family and will always remain a family member. I have my photos loaded on a disc and ready to be mailed but realized I do not have your address. Sorry about that as I am certain it was on some of the items you mailed to me. Please provide that to me and I will get the disc in the mail. Best regards, Clyde."*

Tom and I had a great conversation about life. Prior to the trip, his wife, Kathy, had written to me expressing her gratitude for making the Milwaukee adventure happen. "It probably means more to Tom and his buddies than you will ever know," she wrote.

CHAPTER 10

2018 ST. LOUIS SUPERCROSS

It took a few weeks for me to come down from the cloud I was on. I needed to prepare #49 for the 2018 Supercross events taking place in St. Louis for the upcoming Monster Energy Supercross series. It was less than a month away, and I had given the Nichols brothers a heads-up in case they wanted to see their old bike after so many years.

I already had the thumbs-up from Ray Mungenast and Dave Larsen (museum curator) to display the #49 bike at the Mungenast Automobiles & Motorcycles Museum for their Supercross party. The second event was at The Moto Museum Supercross party later that day. The third event was the Supercross Legends and Heroes display the following day.

One day before the Supercross, I received a package in the mail—from Bill Davidson. Inside was a book and a letter. In the letter Bill reflected on the museum visit and the great job I did on the bike and getting the team together. He also thanked me for the bike stand. The book was one his father Willie G. Davidson had authored, called *Wandering*. Both Bill and Willie had signed the inside cover. It contained Willie's sketches and doodles of motorcycles, decals, logos and the like. I was humbled by such a gift.

The St. Louis Supercross arrived and I invited my dad and father-in-law to join me. The Mungenast museum was a must-see.

When we arrived at the Mungenast Museum, Ray picked a spot out for me in the front entrance of the museum. Jim Simmons and Stan Rubottom showed up. I invited them since I was beginning the preservation on Jim's 1976 ISDT Silver medal Husqvarna. It was fun to watch Ray, Jim, and Stan catch up on old times. Meanwhile, my father and father-in-law toured the museum.

ISDT Legends Jim Simmons and Stan Rubottom at the Mungenast
Museum 2018 Supercross party. Photo by Keith Geisner.

Tom Fox showed up during lunch at the museum. Tom was the administrator of the Harley-Davidson MX Owners group on Facebook. He brought me a poster I had recently purchased from him. It was a copy of a 1978 Cycle World USA race poster in St. Peters, Missouri. The poster mentioned the names of Marty Smith, Roger DeCoster and Broc Glover. It just so happened that Broc Glover was at the museum that day, so I rushed over to Ray to find a Sharpie.

Getting a signature and a picture with Broc Glover at the Mungenast Museum. Photo by Keith Geisner.

I remembered the year before, when Mason Boyd sent me a picture of his Harley-Davidson MX at the Daytona Legends and Heroes display with Broc Glover next to his bike. Mason said Broc gave him crap over not having Dunlop tires on his bike, since Broc works for Dunlop. After Mason told me that story, I sent Broc a message through Facebook to let him know that I was planning on being at the 2018 Supercross events with the #49 bike.

What a day this was turning out to be! At two o'clock my father and father-in-law helped me load up and I headed to the Dome at America's Center to get my pit pass for Supercross the next day.

I felt like a VIP after getting my wrist band and pit pass to the Supercross. Leaving the Dome, I headed over to the Moto Museum for the last stop of the day. I was the second person to bring a bike in for display. The event coordinator wanted the #49 bike to be the center of attention. It was a good thing I brought everything to display. We were able to hang the team members' jerseys above the bike, and the layout looked perfect.

Between setting up the bike and the start of the actual event, I headed to the attached Triumph Grill for a drink. As I sat there talking to various people, I looked to my right and Roger DeCoster was seated right next to me. I took the opportunity and got another signature on my poster. Another awesome highlight of the day!

The Supercross party at the Moto Museum went great. I met Broc Glover again and discussed the #49 bike with him. He was a pleasure to speak with. He knew so much about Marty Tripes and Rex Staten that I learned things I didn't know. He got a kick out of the bike and said I did a perfect job preserving it. He also had to comment on how the front fender was slightly twisted in front. Broc laughed and said that it was an issue they always had, no matter what bike brand it was, that the front fender was slightly twisted. He said mechanics would always have a heat gun or torch out, trying to form the twist out of them. (Note the photo of #11 Rich Eierstedt and the twist in his front fender. Could that be the same front fender on #49?)

Marty Tripes and Rich Eierstedt at the Rabbit Run Trans-AMA. Notice the twist in Rich's #11 fender. Photo by Joseph Savant.

Twist in #49's front fender. Photo by Keith Geisner.

Second picture of the day with Broc Glover at the Moto Museum. Photo by Keith Geisner.

By the time 9 p.m. rolled around I was ready to head home for the night. I loaded up #49 and said my goodbyes—I had a big day tomorrow.

On Saturday I headed back to St. Louis for the Supercross events. I had to walk nearly a mile from where I parked. I started by taking my team bike stand to the area and meeting with the main man of the Legends and Heroes traveling display, Alex Moroz. He gave me a location to set up #49 and my barriers. I spent the next hour setting up and helping Alex set up his area.

It was an awesome experience to be behind the scenes in the pits of a Supercross event. I was able to do a pre-walk of the track with the rest of the Legends and Heroes people and meet Jeff Emig. Being on the track was another incredible experience.

Once I got back to the display area, the general crowd started coming in. The Harley-Davidson Team MX bike got a lot of attention, and throughout the day I answered many questions. As I was sitting there, I noticed a guy come up and stare at the bike. For some reason, I felt compelled to talk to him: it turned out to be Tracy Nichols. Tracy got a kick out of seeing the bike after so many years. I walked him around the bike, pointing out areas of difficulty during the preservation. I was glad Tracy made the trip and reminisced about his racing past.

Tracy Nichols reunites with the #49 bike after bringing it to
Missouri forty years earlier. Photo by Keith Geisner.

My nephew Nathan and cousins Andrew and Adrian DeRousse also dropped in. I loved being able to share this special moment with family. When it was time to load up, I was tired from standing around on concrete all day. I watched the opening ceremony of the Supercross, but I didn't stay long. I was ready for a break and to come down out of the clouds.

I was sad to learn that 2018 was the last time St. Louis would be hosting the Supercross event, but it also made me feel fortunate to get the chance to do what I did over the last year and half. I thought about how time had flown. The end of the St. Louis Supercross would be another asterisk in the motorcycle history books, along with the Harley-Davidson MX team.

AUTHOR'S NOTE

Within a month of the St. Louis Supercross, Sara and I flew out to Portland, Oregon, to catch up with some of her college friends. We hoped to meet up with Tom and Kathy Volin while we were out there, but our paths were too far apart to cross.

Our first stop was a bed and breakfast in McMinnville. It was a nice little town with wineries nearby. Our room had a small library, and as I was ever the early riser, I woke up, had some breakfast, and then sat down to read until Sara and our friends got up.

I decided to read *The Power of Starting Something Stupid*, by Rich and Natalie Norton. It was subtitled, "How to Crush Fear, Make Dreams Happen, and Live Without Regret." Within thirty minutes of reading it, the idea for this book was born. I figured I owed it to the forgotten team members, as well as myself, to take the next step in this journey with #49.

Later, in December of 2018, it was announced that Rex Staten would be inducted into the Trailblazer Hall of Fame, joining his Harley-Davidson mechanic, Steve Storz. When the dates were set for the 75th Annual Trailblazer banquet, Steve Storz emailed me to see if I had any photos of Rex I could send to add to Rex's introduction video and the event program. I had plenty of pics, but since I wasn't the photographer, I had to ask permission. Both Lyndon Fox and Steve Gustafson were happy to donate their photos for the event.

I asked Steve Storz if he could get some photos of Rex Staten signed for me at the event. Steve replied that it wouldn't be a problem, but why didn't I just come out and meet him in person? My wife was all for it and we made plans to go to California. However, I wasn't in a position to haul #49 out there with us, and in a way I was relieved. I could focus on my other goals, like getting Rex's and Steve's signatures on some of my smaller memorabilia. I ended up having one heck of a time getting the 1976 team gas tank through airport TSA. It took some wrangling, but finally I got permission.

When Sara and I landed we met with an old college friend of hers before heading up to Ventura where the next day we would be visiting with Steve Storz. Ventura is a beautiful city and the weather was awesome as we cruised over to Steve's shop around eleven o'clock on Friday morning. It was great to finally meet Steve in person. We hit it off right away, recapping the previous year's experiences and getting to know each other's family and business history. He gave us a shop tour before we went out for lunch. Everything was top-notch. Before leaving Steve's place, he signed my items. I gave him one of the H-D team jerseys and he traded me an official Storz Performance T-shirt. I was secretly hoping I would get one. We said our goodbyes and planned to meet up the next day at the banquet.

Visiting with Steve Storz at Storz Performance. Photo by Keith Geisner.

We drove down to Carson and as soon as we made it to our hotel, I noticed John Penton and family seated in the lobby. My heart skipped a beat. I quickly checked in and then ran out to the car to tell Sara the news. She didn't get my excitement, but she played along as I approached the Pentons for autographs. Jeff, Tom, Jack and John all signed my number plate and posed for pictures with Sara and me. Later, Carl Cranke, Lars Larsson, Chris Carter, and Eric Jenson autographed my number plate as well.

When we arrived at the banquet, my goal was to get Rex Staten as well as Marty Tripes, whom I had seen on the attendee list, to sign my H-D items. We started off having lunch with Steve Storz and his wife, Joanie. Steve had a copy of the event program and I was excited to see the two Lyndon Fox photos and one from Steve Gustafson. They were cited as coming from the "Keith Geisner Collection."

After lunch, I spied Marty in the lobby, but he looked busy so I briefly introduced myself and said that I would love to get his autograph later on.

I was wearing my H-D MX jersey with "Staten #31" on the back. As we entered the bike show and commons area, we started to walk the perimeter of the display area. I saw Rex on the opposite side and he waved to me. To say I was nervous would be a tremendous understatement. Rex already had a crowd of people around him. As we got closer, his wife, Lynn, came up to me and said Rex was looking forward to meeting me and that he had brought his jersey as well. Rex came up behind Lynn and shook my hand. We hit it off right away. I pulled out my photo book of the #49 bike and we paged through it, telling stories. I had the tank and other items in the trunk of my car, so we went out to see my items and Rex went to retrieve his jersey.

Rex made me feel like part of the team. Photo by Keith Geisner.

As Rex examined and signed my items, I admired his team H-D MX jersey. How exciting was that to hold a real team jersey? He then put it on and proceeded to get pictures taken with me. We had a good time talking, but I felt bad because a line of people wanting to talk to Rex was forming. We said our goodbyes until later.

While waiting for Marty Tripes to come over, I was able to meet Tommy Croft and get his autograph. After a while, there were still no signs of Marty and it was getting close to the time we needed to go back to the room to change for dinner. I was getting nervous, but I decided if I had to, I would take the tank to dinner with me.

Making lifelong friends at the 75th annual Trailblazer's Banquet. Photo by Keith Geisner.

As luck would have it, I found Marty at the hotel restaurant. He kindly signed my items and talked about his days on the MX team. I thanked him for his time and told him I'd be in touch. It had taken me two and a half years to finally meet the man.

When we re-entered the bike show area, I spied Bob Hannah, so I motioned Sara over to the side, where I prepared a number plate, a photo of Hannah and Kudalski, and a marker. The photo was a perfect icebreaker. Before I could hand him my Sharpie, Bob pulled out his own and signed my items. It was short and sweet, but he was welcoming. I shook his hand and thanked him.

Don Kudalski and Bob Hannah battle it out at the New Orleans
Supercross, 1978. Photo by Barcroft Media Limited.

We met back up with Rex and his wife, Lynn. He was such a nice guy. I started telling him about the stories I'd heard about him through my research, and he shared his own stories with me. As I said my goodbyes, I saw Rex as more of a lifelong friend than some photo I had been studying for the past couple of years.

I made my way into the dining hall to find Sara. She was already acquainted with the motorcycle legends sitting with us at our table, and she proceeded to introduce me to them. The banquet was an awesome experience. I went on to meet and get autographs from Malcolm Smith, Brad Lackey and Mert Lawwill.

Rex's video and presentation were excellent and included images from Lyndon Fox. At the end, Sara and I made our way back over to the hotel. I'm so glad I took Steve's advice and attended this wonderful event. Sara and I made some great friends and lasting memories. Looking back, I never would have imagined the journey #49 has taken me on. I only hope future generations of motorcycle enthusiasts preserve the past as much as present day.

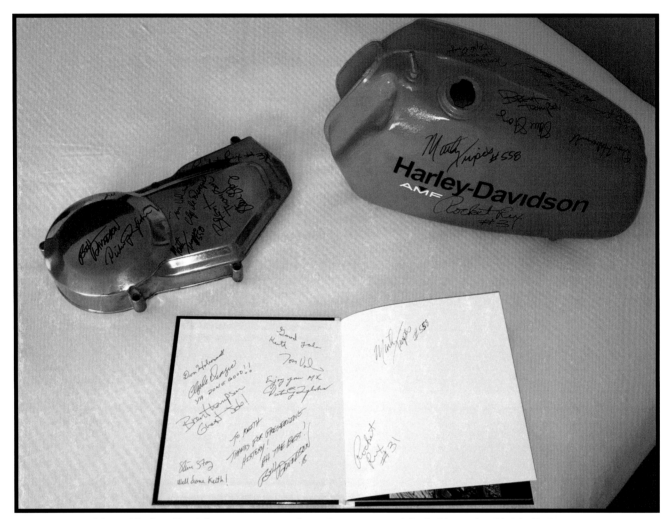

More Harley-Davidson team member signatures added. Photo by Keith Geisner.

IN CLOSING

What does the future hold for #49? I'm not letting go of my lottery ticket anytime soon. I have a goal to meet as many of the team members as possible, including a visit with #49 himself, Don Kudalski. From my perspective, preserving #49 was only one step in the journey—meeting the people behind the bike and hearing about their experiences and passion for the sport has been the real adventure.

I also plan to continue showing the bike at special events. There are few things I enjoy more than spending an afternoon with fellow enthusiasts talking about bikes. I've met so many great people, whether riding, racing, or simply walking through a motorcycle museum. Who knows, maybe #49 will even end up on loan to a museum someday....

THE HARLEY-DAVIDSON MOTOCROSS TEAM STATS AND PHOTOS

The below team stats were found online in the *Cycle News* West Archives. I'm positive the team raced more events than those listed below. If a rider didn't place within the top twenty, or did not finish (DNF), there was usually no mention of him being at that event.

From 1972 through 1978, the Harley-Davidson MX race department was busy designing, testing, and competing with their 250cc and 341cc MX motorcycles. One of the earliest examples of a Harley-Davidson MX prototype was test-ridden by Ken Johnson. Scott Wallenberg said that Ken was also testing the rear fork suspension on 350 H-D Sprints. There was not much racing taking place in 1974; however, the race department was still busy designing and test riding with Mike Lewis and Terry Clark. No sooner did 1975 kick off, Mike set out to represent Harley-Davidson as their first factory rider of the unofficial team.

That's Mike Lewis racing the Harley-Davidson factory 250cc MXer, that is constantly undergoing changes. Shown here at the Aztalan Grand Prix in Lake Mills, Wisconsin, the machine sports trick suspension, but the trickest thing may be that team jersey (in orange and balck, natch) Mike's wearing. Hey Harley, how much?

First Harley-Davidson MX team rider Mike Lewis captured by *Cycle News*. Photo provided by *Cycle News*.

This same year, Harley-Davidson released a small quantity of production MX bikes to the public. The first official race of the MX250 production bike was by Sonny Defeo in Herman, Nebraska, on June 1, 1975. His race was cut short when his bike had an electrical failure. And we can't forget the two-page spread in the October 21, 1975 edition of *Cycle News*, where privateer Ricky Pilgrim #141V was photographed riding his MX250, sponsored by San Marcos Harley-Davidson of Texas. (See later pic of Ricky's MX250 fitted with upper fork accumulators. This was proof that select racers were getting Harley-Davidson race department support.)

Rex Marsee's comment after I sent him the Ricky Pilgrim article out of *Cycle News*: "Keith, this article verifies what I have said all along, the first build was close to 100, but Clyde Denzer ran short on some parts, I believe, and the rest of the planned production was not finished, so only about 90 were built. Many say 45 to 50 were built, actually that was not true. A second hundred build was scheduled, but never built in Milwaukee. Rex."

Cycle News coverage of Ricky Pilgrim. Photo provided by *Cycle News*.

#141V, Ricky Pilgrim with canister front forks, possible factory support. Photo by James LaPaz.

Even though a Harley-Davidson team was not established yet, the race department was still developing the bike with help from their test riders, Wayne Welzien and Eric Skrudland. By the end of the 1975 season, Harley-Davidson would be in talks with Rex Staten to team up with Eric Skrudland, planning their motocross team attack for 1976.

The 1976 season started off with the newly formed Harley-Davidson MX team competing in the Winter-AMA series in Florida, where there would be five rounds. The newly signed Rex Staten started off on fire, if you consider the fact the motorcycle he was racing was new to the game. Rex was joined by Eric Skrudland, who, after the first Winter-AMA race, injured his foot and was done for the season. Mechanics were Don Habermehl and Tim Dixon. After Eric left the team, Ricky O'Brien was the next rider to join. By the second round, Rex Staten gave the Harley-Davidson team their first moto victory, with a (1-4) performance in Orlando, finishing with an overall third place. The final round in Cocoa Beach had Rex placing third overall with newly signed Ricky O'Brien finishing twelfth place overall. Rex took third overall in the Winter-AMA series. Harley-Davidson had made its statement in motocross!

2/1/76 - Jacksonville, FL Winter-AMA: Staten (DNF–3), out of the top 20. Engine failure.
2/8/76 - Orlando, FL Winter-AMA: Staten, (1–4) for a 3rd overall and Harley-Davidson's first moto win in history.
2/15/76 - Gainesville, FL Winter-AMA: Staten (out of the top 20). Broken chain.

2/22/76 - St. Petersburg, FL Winter-AMA: Staten (4–5) 5th overall.

2/29/76 - Cocoa Beach, FL Winter-AMA: Staten (5–4) for a 3rd overall, Ricky O'Brien 12th. Rex took 3rd overall in the 76 Winter-AMA series.

3/6/76 - Daytona, FL Supercross: Staten took 24th overall.

3/26-27/76 - Pontiac, MI Supercross IV: Staten went (6–7–3–3) for a 5th overall.

4/4/76 - Rancho Cordova, CA: Staten suffered ignition problems all day and settled with 12th.

4/11/76 - Phoenix, AZ: Staten went (15–11) for a 12th overall.

4/25/76 - Houston, TX Rio Bravo MX Park: Staten (10–11) 8th overall.

5/2/76 - Forsyth, GA Towaliga River Cycle Park: Staten took 25th overall.

5/23/76 - Fogelsville, PA 250 National: Staten (19–14) 14th overall.

6/1/76 - News that Mike Gillman debuted the new 341cc H-D MX at the Allenton, PA National riding for the support class. (*Cycle News* 6/1/76)

6/25/76 - Carlsbad, CA USGP 500cc: Staten debuted the 341cc HD and went (14–DNF) 18th overall.

7/18/76 - St. Peters, MO 250 support: Ricky O'Brien (5–14) 9th overall.

7/24/76 - Los Angeles, CA Superbowl: Staten 13th overall.

8/1/76 - New Berlin, NY Unadilla: Staten (7–18) for a 13th overall 500cc.

8/8/76 - Carlsbad, CA CMC MX: Staten did not place.

8/15/76 - New Castle, KY: Staten went (9–13) for 9th overall.

8/6/76 - Irwindale, CA CMC Night National MX: Staten took first in the 250 pro class.

9/5-12/76 - Trophy des Nations, Netherlands: Staten raced for the USA–5th place.

10/3/76 - Axton, VA: Staten (18–11) for 14th overall.

12/4/76 - Anaheim, CA American MX Final: Staten 12th overall.

This picture was taken the day Rex Staten won Harley-Davidson's first moto ever. Photo by Doug Hill.

Rex Staten #46, 1976, the day Rex won H-D's first moto at the Winter-AMA. Photo by Doug Hill.

"Rocket" Rex had engine problems in the first moto with his new Harley, but in the second moto finished third.

Rex #46 1976 Round 1 Winter-AMA. Photo provided by *Cycle News.*

Rex #46 1976 Pontiac Silverdome. Photo by Jeff Holzhausen.

Rex #46 1976 Unadilla Trans-AMA. Photo by Lyndon Fox.

Rex #46 1976 Unadilla Trans-AMA. Photo by Lyndon Fox.

Rex #46 1976 at Unadilla. Photo by Lyndon Fox.

Rex #46 1976 at Unadilla. Photo by Lyndon Fox.

Rex #17 at the 1976 Superbowl. Photo by Mark Kiel.

Rex #46 1976 at Unadilla. Photo by Lyndon Fox.

Rex #46 1976 Unadilla Trans-AMA. Photo by Lyndon Fox.

Rex #46 1976 at Unadilla. Photo by Lyndon Fox.

Rex Staten #22 USGP 1976, MX360. Photo by Phil Davy.

The year 1977 brought a new face to the team. Marty Tripes joined Rex Staten for the season. Rex took eighth overall in the 500cc National MX series. Rich Eierstedt joined the team to race the Trans-AMA series in the last quarter of 1977. Marty finished in the top ten three times during the Trans-AMA series. The team would switch to the last configuration of their team bikes by mid-season. The changes consisted of a new frame by C&J, a Cross Up swingarm, Fox air shocks, and KYB front forks.

1/30/77 - Orange County, CA CMC Saddleback: Staten took 3rd in the 500 pro.

2/6/77 - AMC Carlsbad MX: Tripes 4th overall.

2/13/77 - Carlsbad, CA CMC: Staten 2nd in the 500 pro and Tripes DNF.

2/27/77 - Orlando, FL (4th round Winter-AMA): Tripes and Staten not in top 20.

3/5/77 - Atlanta, GA Supercross: Tripes 10th, Staten 12th.

4/10/77 - Plymouth, CA Hangtown 250MX National opener: Tripes 4th, Staten 13th.

4/17/77 - Lebanon, TN 250 National: Tripes 16th, Staten 17th.

4/13/77 - San Diego, CA CMC HSMX: Tripes 1st 250 pro.

4/24/77 - Herman, NE Omaha Moto Park: Staten 18th.

4/27/77 - San Diego, CA CMC HSMX: Tripes 3rd 250 pro.

5/1/77 - Southwick, MA Moto-X383, 250 National: Tripes 18th, Staten 21st.

5/15/77 - Lake Sugar Tree MX Park, VA 250 National: Tripes 12th.

5/22/77 - Buchanan, MI 250 National: Staten 11th.

5/29/77 - Morris, PA High Point 250 National: Staten 13th, Tripes 14th.

6/19/77 - Carlsbad, CA USGP: Staten 9th, Tripes 16th.

7/9/77 - Los Angeles, CA Superbowl: Tripes 10th, Staten 13th.

7/17/77 - Lake Whitney, TX 500 National: Staten 10th.

7/24/77 - St. Peters, MO Cycle World USA, 500 National: Staten: 8th.

7/27/77 - Chula Vista, CA South Bay CMC: Tripes 1st 250 Pro.

7/31/77 - New Berlin, NY Unadilla 500 National: Staten 3rd (raced the 341cc with a 250 tank decal).

8/3/77 - Chula Vista, CA South Bay CMC: Tripes 2nd 250 pro. (Bike prepared by Vey's Motorcycle Enterprises)

8/7/77 - Charlotte, NC 500 National: Staten 16th.

8/21/77 - Dallas, GA 500 National: Staten 9th, Tripes 21st.

8/28/77 - St. Petersburg, FL Final round of 500 National: Staten 9th, Tripes 12th.

9/4/77 - Sunnymead, CA CRC: Staten 250 Pro–DNF.

9/9/77 - Corona Night MX: Staten 2nd 250 Pro.

9/17-18/77- Irvine/Orange County, CA Olympiad: Tripes 10th overall on 341cc.

9/25/77 - Lexington, OH (Round 1 Trans-AMA): Tripes 9th, Staten 16th.

10/2/77 - Axton, VA (Round 2 Trans-AMA): Staten 19th, Tripes DNF.

10/9/77 - New Berlin, NY (Round 3 Trans-AMA): Staten 16th.

10/16/77 - Buchanan, MI (Round 4 Trans-AMA): Tripes 6th.

10/23/77 - St. Peters, MO (Round 5 Trans-AMA): Tripes 12th, Eierstedt 15th.

10/30/77 - Plano, TX (Round 6 Trans-AMA): Tripes 14th, Staten 16th.

11/5/77 - Puyallup, WA (Round 7 Trans-AMA): Eierstedt 11th, Staten 18th.

11/12/77 - Anaheim, CA Coca Cola MX Final: Tripes 6th, Staten 11th.

11/30/77 - Sonoma, CA (Trans-AMA Final): Eierstedt 11th, Tripes 20th.

**HARLEY-DAVIDSON MOTOCROSS TEAM RACER,
REX STATEN--FAST AND STYLISH.**

Rex was the face of the Harley-Davidson MX team. Used with
permission of the Harley-Davidson Archives.

1977 Trans-AMA, Rex Staten #31 and Marty Tripes #588. Last version of the team bike. Rex's bike is fitted with a Thor swingarm. Photo by Jim Gianatsis/FastDates.com.

1977 Trans-AMA, #588 Marty Tripes, Texas Rabbit Run. Photo by Joseph Savant.

1977 Trans-AMA, #588 Marty Tripes at Lake Whitney. Photo by Jim Gianatsis/FastDates.com.

Rex Staten #31 racing at Unadilla in the 500 National 1977. Photo by Lyndon Fox.

#31 Rex Staten Southwick.1977. Photo by Lyndon Fox.

1977, Rex Staten wrenching on his own #31 with Don Habermehl next to him. Photo by Lyndon Fox.

1977 #558 Marty Tripes at Southwick. Photo by Lyndon Fox.

1977 #558 Marty Tripes at Southwick. Photo by Lyndon Fox.

1977 #558 Marty Tripes. Photo by Lyndon Fox.

1977 #31, Rex Staten at Southwick. Photo by Lyndon Fox.

#558 Marty Tripes, 1977 500 National. Photo by Jim Gianatsis/FastDates.com.

1977 Winter-AMA, #558 Tripes. Notice the Don Habermehl-shaved cylinder. Photo by Lyndon Fox.

1977 Winter-AMA, Habermehl working on Tripes' bike. Photo by Lyndon Fox.

1977 Winter-AMA, Marty Tripes. Photo by Lyndon Fox.

1977 Winter-AMA, #31 Rex Staten. Photo by Lyndon Fox.

1977 Winter-AMA, #558 Marty Tripes. Photo by Lyndon Fox.

1977 TRANS-AMA, #558 Marty Tripes. Photo by Lyndon Fox.

1977 #31 Rex Staten at Unadilla. Photo by Lyndon Fox.

1977 TRANS-AMA, #558 Marty Tripes. Photo by Lyndon Fox.

1977 Winter-AMA, #558 Marty Tripes. Photo by Lyndon Fox.

1977 Winter-AMA, #558 Marty Tripes. Photo by Lyndon Fox.

1977 Winter-AMA, #558 Marty Tripes. Photo by Lyndon Fox.

1977 500 National Unadilla, #31 Rex Staten. Photo by Lyndon Fox.

1977 500 National Unadilla, #31 Rex Staten. Photo by Lyndon Fox.

1977 Marty Tripes participating in the Olympiad. Photo by Mark Kiel.

1977 Marty Tripes participating in the Olympiad. Photo by Mark Kiel.

1977 Marty Tripes participating in the Olympiad. Dirt tracking! Photo by Mark Kiel.

Rich Eierstedt #11 at the 1977 Superbowl. Notice the Dunlop sticker on the side number plate is the same one on #49's swingarm. Photo by Mark Kiel.

1977 Marty Tripes Superbowl. Rare right-hand-exiting exhaust with Fox shocks and possible race department-made black swingarm. Photo by Mark Kiel.

1977 Rex Staten Superbowl. Photo by Mark Kiel.

At the end of the 1977 Trans-AMA series, Marty Tripes, Rex Staten, and Rich Eierstedt all cut ties with the Harley-Davidson MX team. Before Christmas, Rex was already riding for Yamaha and Marty was in talks with Honda. Don Habermehl and Tim Dixon were moving on to other things. Don started supporting flat-track racing inside the race department and Tim left the company. That left manager Clyde Denzer, mechanic Tom Volin and engineer John Ingham to see what they could put together for the 1978 season.

The 1978 MX season started out slowly. The team missed the first two rounds of the Winter-AMA series, trying to sign rider Mickey Boone, who turned down Harley-Davidson's offer and went to race for Suzuki. Like they say, everything happens for a reason, because during round three of the Winter-AMA series in Jacksonville, the team reached out to the experienced—and teamless—rider Don Kudalski. Don was already winning the 500cc class of the Winter-AMA series aboard his Yamaha YZ400. This may have been what caught Harley-Davidson's attention. Regardless of what brought them together, on February 19th, 1978, Don's first race aboard the Harley-Davidson MX250 ended with him winning in the 250cc class, giving H-D their first major MX win. This would be #49's best finish of the year, but that didn't mean Don and mechanic Tom Volin didn't give everyone a run for their money. Don and Tom traveled together for the 1978 season, racing leftover bikes from the 1977 Trans-AMA series with the 250cc motor. Also, this would be the year when the Harley-Davidson MX race team would debut their water-cooled MX250 at the 250 Red Bud MX National in Buchanan, Michigan—a design project run by John Ingham. Sadly, this would be Harley-Davidson's last MX season. The team would close their doors at the end of 1978 and the rest is MX history.

2/19/78 - Jacksonville, FL Winter-AMA: Kudalski 1st place.

2/26/78 - St. Petersburg, FL Winter-AMA Final round: Kudalski 13th.

3/4/78 - Atlanta, GA Superbowl: Kudalski DNF, due to mechanical issues.

3/12/78 - Daytona Beach, FL Toyota Supercross series: Kudalski not in the top 20.

3/17/78 - Houston, TX Supercross (Round 4): Kudalski DNF, out with injury.

4/30/78 - Herman, NE 250 MX Nationals: Kudalski 16th.

5/7/78 - Southwick, MA 250 MX Nationals, (Round 5): Kudalski 6th.

5/13/78 - Pittsburgh, PA 3 Rivers Stadium Supercross: Kudalski 8th in the consolation.

5/21/78 - New Orleans, LA Supercross: Kudalski 11th.

5/28/78 - Waco, TX 250 Nationals: Kudalski 14th.

7/2/78 - Buchanan, MI Red Bud MX 250 National: Kudalski DNF, water-cooled bike placed outside top 20 riders; Rider #383 Tracy Nichols.

#49 Don "Killer" Kudalski final round of the Winter-AMA. Photo by Jim Gianatsis/FastDates.com.

Kudalski makes history

125cc class winner Mark Barnett carefully picks his line around Chip Watts.

By Jim Gianatsis

JACKSONVILLE, FL, FEB. 19

After years of trying, Harley-Davidson finally recorded their name at the top of a score sheet in National caliber motocross. The rider that put them there in race number three of the MXL sponsored Florida Winter-AMA Series held at Action Park Motocross was none other than the "Killer," Florida's Don Kudalski. Don used the day to continue his domination of the Open class with his Gordon Rainbow tuned Yamaha for the third week in a row, and also entered the 250cc class in a test ride to determine if he should sign on with Harley as their only factory motocross rider. When Don walked off with the 250cc class as well on the Tom Volin prepared CR 250, the contracts were ready to be signed.

Kudalski's Harley ride came about after Mickey Boone turned down his supposedly lucrative sponsorship with the Milwaukee firm at the first race of the Florida Series because the bike "...just wasn't competitive." While Don obviously thought it was, Mickey turned up at the races this weekend with a van load of new RM production Suzukis and word was that he had picked up Suzuki B Team support for the coming season. Marty Moates also revealed that he had picked up sponsorship from LOP to campaign LOP modified Suzukis in the Supercross Series and 125cc Nationals.

Rain had saturated the soil at Action Motocross Park, turning the track surface into one of the strangest ever seen in motocross. The solid black, sticky sand was like wet, shredded foam rubber, building tricky berms and ruts that recoiled and flexed every time a rider got near.

125cc Professional

For the third week in a row 17-year-old Mark Johnson wrenched production Team Suzuki RM Type II to victory circle for certain victory in the Series championship. But it was hardly an easy ride.

"I crashed three times in that last moto," moaned Mark as he rubbed his sore fanny. In the opening moto though, he had it simple enough.

Hammering away at his shifter Mark swooped out his first holeshot of the day ahead of Bill Joyce, Pat Moroney, Kippy Pierce and FMF's Gregg Toyama. Quickly the pressure slackened as Yamaha support rider Pierce highsided his bike over a rubber berm and dived into one of the track's three-foot-deep infield ponds. Bill Joyce's luck wasn't much better as the berms knocked off his exhaust pipe on the second lap as he tried to shorten the distance on Barnett. Soon Pat Moroney was the only rider left in Mark's wake, but Pat was being left behind by Mark as Mike Guerra closed up and took over second spot. Part of the problem was that Moroney kept pitching his chain.

Kippy Pierce was making up for lost time spent in the drink and worked his way all the way up from the back of the pack to spectacularly pass both Toyama and Moroney on the last lap for third place. Georgia's Johnny Borders collected sixth.

The second moto needed a restart after everyone jumped the flagman (the starting gate was buried under two feet of mud).

Kudalski making Harley-Davidson MX history his first race aboard the bike. Photo provided by *Cycle News*.

March 8, 1978 **CYCLE NEWS**

The Winter-AMA champs: Don Kudalski (49), John Calathes and Mark Barnett (24) pose with their mechanics.

Kudalski's second race for the H-D team. He locks in the win of the 500cc Winter-AMA class on his YZ400 wearing his H-D gear. Took 13th on this H-D MX250. Photo provided by *Cycle News*.

Don Kudalski at Rio Bravo, TX 1978. Photo by Tommy Montgomery.

Nichols and the Harley-Davidson water-cooled bike debut. Photo by Jim Gianatsis/FastDates.com.

In memory of John Ingham
(1939-2019)

Don Habermehl, John Ingham and Marty Tripes, 1977 Winter-
AMA. Photo by Jim Gianatsis/FastDates.com.

Printed in the United States
By Bookmasters